CW00504869

HAUNTED
ST ALBANS

HAUNTED
ST ALBANS

Paul Adams

The
History
Press

For Eddie Brazil,
to mark ten years of friendship.

First published 2013

The History Press
The Mill, Brimscombe Port
Stroud, Gloucestershire, GL5 2QG
www.thehistorypress.co.uk

Reprinted 2016

© Paul Adams, 2013

The right of Paul Adams to be identified as the Author
of this work has been asserted in accordance with the
Copyright, Designs and Patents Act 1988.

All rights reserved. No part of this book may be reprinted
or reproduced or utilised in any form or by any electronic,
mechanical or other means, now known or hereafter invented,
including photocopying and recording, or in any information
storage or retrieval system, without the permission in writing
from the Publishers.

British Library Cataloguing in Publication Data.
A catalogue record for this book is available from the British Library.

ISBN 978 0 7524 6547 0

Typesetting and origination by The History Press
Printed in Great Britain

CONTENTS

ACKNOWLEDGEMENTS

A number of people deserve recognition for their help with the writing of this book, and my grateful thanks go to the following: Bill King, historian and investigator for the Luton Paranormal Society (LPS) for writing the foreword and for his interest in the project; Eddie Brazil, who once again has provided superb contemporary illustrations and has followed the progress of this particular book with his usual much-needed enthusiasm and humour; Peter Underwood, for providing access to his files on Hertfordshire and St Albans hauntings; Natalie Dearman from the *Herts Advertiser*, for help with collecting new local paranormal encounters; the late Tony Broughall, for allowing me to quote from his published memoirs; Juliet Milton for permission to reproduce material from the Mountfitchet Castle website; David Thorold and Catherine Newley from the Museum of St Albans who assisted with photographs and the checking of historical data; Damien O'Dell of the Anglia Paranormal Investigation Society (APIS), who allowed me to use material from his published accounts of the city's numerous hauntings; Tom Ruffles, for helping with statistical information on Britian's ghost hunters; and Peter Baker, who assisted with research into the history of St Albans. I would also like to thank all the residents of St Albans and others, including Mary Myers and Jo Clarke, who have contacted and shared with me some of their unique experiences of the city's ghosts, and also Nicola Guy and Chris Ogle at The History Press for efficiently seeing this book through to publication. Finally, special thanks go as always to Aban, Idris, Isa and Sakina, for their patience and inspiration, as well as remembering our Saturday morning St Albans outings.

ABOUT THE AUTHOR

PAUL ADAMS was born in Epsom, Surrey in 1966 and has been interested in the paranormal since the mid-1970s. Employed as a draughtsman in the UK construction industry for thirty years, he has worked in three haunted buildings but has yet to see a true ghost. As well as the history of psychical research, his main interests at present are in materialisation mediumship and the physical phenomena of Spiritualism. He has contributed articles to several specialist paranormal periodicals and acted as editor and publisher for *Two Haunted Counties*, the memoirs of Luton ghost hunter, Tony Broughall. Adams is the co-author of *The Borley Rectory Companion*, *Shadows in the Nave* and *Extreme Hauntings*, and has written *Haunted Luton and Dunstable* and *Ghosts & Gallows*, a study of British true crime cases with paranormal connections. He is also an amateur mycologist and viola-player and has lived in Luton since 2006. Details of books and contact information can be found at www.pauladamsauthor.co.uk.

FOREWORD

IN 2008, a survey of 2,060 people revealed that nearly 4 out of 10 people believed in ghosts. This was almost identical to the results of a survey carried out ten years previously, yet it was a fourfold increase over the results of a Gallup poll from 1950, when only 1 in 10 said they believed in the paranormal (with 1 in 50 reporting that they had actually encountered a ghost). I have met people who have seen ghosts, and I have had my own encounters with the paranormal, especially during my years with the Luton Paranormal Society (LPS). After investigating nearly 300 sites in Hertfordshire, Bedfordshire and Buckinghamshire, as well as places as far afield as Edinburgh, Gloucester, Norwich and Winchester, I have found that ghosts can be seen at any time of day, in any location, and by more than one person at the same time, so there has to be something beyond the claims that the sightings are just being down to people's imagination.

As a local author with an extensive knowledge of the hauntings of the Three Counties, I know St Albans well and I am aware of how haunted a place it is; yet Paul Adams has managed to find even more hauntings for his book *Haunted St Albans*. Many ghost stories are anecdotal or even apocryphal, their origins are obscure and many just sound

St Albans' medieval clock tower, starting point for the city ghost walk in Chapter 6. (Paul Adams)

like tales passed down through the years, accompanied by the usual embellishments which plague such tales. Not so with many of Paul's reports, many of which are either first-hand, or recorded decades ago by Bedfordshire's proficient and pioneering ghost hunter, Tony Broughall.

I think it would be fair to say that there are many strange things out there which, so far, science has failed to explain. Within this book are a large number of these inexplicable occurrences, taken from a city which comes 38th out of the 51 English cities by population, yet has what is fast approaching 100 haunted sites; many more than its fair share, some would say. With full details and extensive background information, these well written reports will interest the hardened ghost investigator like myself, people interested in the history of St Albans and even the eternal sceptic. Enjoy!

William H. King

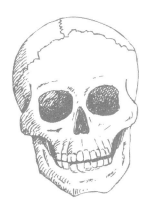

INTRODUCTION

IN early December 1869, two Cambridge intellectuals, Henry Sidgwick and Frederick W.H. Myers, took an evening walk under the stars. At some point their conversation turned to 'those faculties of man, real or supposed, which appear to be inexplicable on any generally recognised hypothesis', a subject that today we recognise more familiarly under the broad label of the 'paranormal'. The seeds of their discussions bore fruit thirteen years later with the 1882 founding of the Society for Psychical Research in London, a ground-breaking organisation that took seriously the study of what up until that time had been considered as fantasy, romance or even heresy: ghosts and apparitions, haunted houses, prophetic dreams and mediumship, subjects that in our own times are perhaps no less controversial, but thanks to the 'occult revolution' of the 1960s, are more easily discussed and now accepted by many.

Whether ghost hunting has finally become a respectable past-time is open to debate. Thanks to an avalanche of reality television programmes on satellite and cable TV, catalysed by the pioneering *Most Haunted*, which first aired in May 2002 and survived fourteen series over eight years including several sensational live specials and spin-off programmes, many hundreds of people around Britain

Frederick W.H. Myers (1843-1901), one of the early pioneers of organised psychical research in England.

have become interested in paranormal investigation and have either joined established regional organisations or set up local groups of their own. According to writer and researcher Damien O'Dell, these psychical groups have a shelf-life of around six to eighteen months, while in 2006, parapsychologist Dr Ciarán O'Keeffe estimated that 1200 separate paranormal societies were active in the country at any one time, involving approximately an astonishing 5,000 amateur researchers and investigators; something that would probably have astounded Victorian psychical researchers such as the pioneering Sidgwick and Myers back in the 1880s.

Many people from all walks of life claim to have had paranormal experiences, often those who have no particular or continuing interest in the subject, the most common and familiar being encounters with ghosts and hauntings. From the vast amount of material that has been issued in both popular and specialist publications, beginning with the Society for Psychical Research's landmark *Phantasms of the Living* in 1886, researchers have established a pattern in the way that people 'see' or encounter ghosts, to the extent that it is possible to assign these spontaneous experiences as belonging to one (or sometimes more than one) broad classification for which tentative but ultimately un-provable explanations have been put forward. In his book *The Ghost Hunter's Guide* (1986), Peter Underwood, one of our most experienced and respected investigators, divides ghost sightings and hauntings into nine separate categories which are still as relevant today as they were when this study was written. Leaving aside what can best be described as the induced phenomena

associated with mediumship and séances, this classification is as follows: atmospheric photograph ghosts (also known as mental imprint manifestations), historical or traditional ghosts, cyclic or recurring ghosts, modern ghosts, ghosts of the living, crisis apparitions (including death bed visions), family ghosts, haunted objects and fraudulent hauntings.

As well as categorisation, it should be mentioned that an encounter with a ghost or apparition does not automatically equate to proof of survival or life after death, in much the same way that a sighting of an unidentified object or UFO in the sky is not proof of the existence of alien spaceships. This tends to often divide researchers of the paranormal into two broad camps: survivalists (believers in some form of afterlife) and non-survivalists (those who consider the mind to be a product of brain function which ends at death), who use evidence gathered from their own particular investigations and studies to support their opposing beliefs.

Investigators who are mediums or use mediums to add a psychic dimension to a ghost hunt are more likely to assign apparitions and similar phenomena as being discarnate personalities or unquiet spirits of the dead. However, there are some parapsychologists who eschew a belief in a spirit world and survival after death; they propose an alternative explanation for the information obtained from mediums and psychics, one that American researcher Hornell Hart termed 'Super ESP' (also known as 'super-psi'). This involves theoretical projections or reservoirs of human consciousness that psychically endowed persons are able to tap into unconsciously in order to obtain supernormal information.

Where the appearance of ghosts and apparitions is concerned, many non-survivalists credit what has become popularly known as the stone tape theory and which forms the basis of Underwood's atmospheric photograph ghost category mentioned above. Originally coined by Cambridge don T.C. (Tom) Lethbridge, a radical twentieth-century psychical researcher dubbed generously by writer Colin Wilson as the 'Einstein of the paranormal', the stone tape proposes the ability of a building or certain set of surroundings to record the psychic impressions of former occupants or happenings, which are then played back or recreated at some future time in the presence of a suitably psychic person. That we all have some inherent psychic ability, albeit to a greater or lesser degree, is shown by the fact that during a paranormal incident in a haunted building or location, one person may see a ghostly form or figure, while at the same time, his or her companion may only detect a drop in temperature or observe a shadowy shape rather than a full-form apparition. A keen and experienced dowser, Tom Lethbridge felt that the presence of water could be a key factor in certain paranormal experiences, a theory that he included – as well as other forays into the unknown – in two books written in the early 1960s, *Ghost and Ghoul* (1961) and *Ghost and Divining Rod* (1963), both of which are of interest to the serious researcher.

Where many old and ancient buildings survive collectively in a given location, the stone tape or atmospheric photograph is then perhaps the most natural non-survivalist explanation for many ghostly and supernatural happenings.

For the city of St Albans, a location with an impressive and enviable association with history and antiquity, it may be the reason for many of the remarkable supernatural encounters that we will be looking at in this book. As a category of alleged haunting, it is one I intend to make a strong case for throughout the present survey.

According to Dr Mark Freeman in *St Albans: A History*, the first known urban settlement near what is now modern St Albans dates from the first century BC. This was a substantial Iron Age town known as Verlamion, which occupied the site of present day Prae Wood, 1.5 miles west of the city centre on the north side of the A4147. The site was excavated by the Scottish-born archaeologist Sir Mortimer Wheeler and his wife in the 1930s and their work, together with more recent studies, have shown Verlamion to have been a thriving agricultural-dependant community with a large cemetery. In AD 43, Emperor Claudius invaded Britain and established Roman rule across the province. The original settlement of Verlamion was developed into a major Roman town, one of the largest in the country, and renamed Verulamium. The Romans paved the ancient Watling Street trackway and relocated the settlement from the higher ground around Prae Wood eastwards to the valley floor, closer to the River Ver. In AD 61, the leader of the Iceni tribe, Queen Boudicca (or Boadicea) lead an organised revolt against the Roman occupiers. During the conflict, the town of Verulamium was sacked and a fire destroyed many of the buildings. Existing records show that the Iceni queen's last known location before her death was the area

The stone tape theory is one explanation for the appearance of ghosts and phantom figures. Here, a spectral monk seemingly materialises in the ruins of haunted Minsden Chapel in Hertfordshire. (Tony Broughall Collection)

around modern day St Albans itself. Although the actual site of her defeat is unknown, it seems likely that Boudicca followed the Watling Street road north and made her last stand at Cuttle Mill close to the village of Paulerspury in Northamptonshire. Following the rebellion, Roman Verulamium recovered and in time became an extensive walled town with a theatre and houses equipped with under-floor heating. The Watling Street highway from Canterbury entered the town walls through the eastern London Gate and departed to the north-east from the Chester Gate over the River Ver.

Queen Boudicca, whose revolution against the occupying Roman forces ended at the Battle of Watling Street. Stories of ghostly figures associated with her uprising occur in at least two Hertfordshire locations.

The Roman presence lasted for over four centuries, during which time the execution of the pagan martyr Alban around AD 250 was the catalyst that lead to the establishment of the city as it is known today. The Anglo-Saxon king Offa of Mercia – said to have received the command to erect a shrine for the relics of St Alban in an angelic vision to atone for the murder of the East Anglian king Ethelbert by his wife Quendreda – is the traditional figure behind the founding of St Albans Abbey in AD 793, but it seems likely that the area was known as a place of pilgrimage many years before the death of Alban himself. Offa and his son, King Egfrith, endowed the monastery, a Benedictine order, with 60,000 acres in south-west Hertfordshire along with additional land in neighbouring Buckinghamshire. As the religious house grew to be the centre of the local economic community, the town of St Albans established itself and grew up around the abbey building; Domesday Book of 1086 gives the number of inhabitants to be around 500 people.

During the course of our survey we will encounter many other aspects of St Albans' long and detailed history – the famines of the mid-thirteenth century, the execution of the rebel leader John Ball during the Peasants' Revolt in 1381, as well as the bloody battles associated with the Wars of the Roses in the fifteenth century. All these events and many others appear to have left their mark in the psychic fabric of this pleasant English city, and we will be examining the evidence for many of the area's historical hauntings in the pages that follow. In 2008, the Revd Lionel Fanthorpe, a well-regarded researcher into psychical subjects and the current (as of 2012) President of the Association for the Scientific Study of Anomalous Phenomena (ASSAP), compiled a comprehensive survey of haunted locations across the British Isles which established St Albans' paranormal pedigree. Fanthorpe's *Supernatural Britain Report* concluded that the city was the fifth most haunted in the country, with eight ghost sightings for every 10,000 citizens.

For *Haunted St Albans*, the first dedicated guide to the city's hauntings in twenty-five years, I have used a similar layout for my survey of the neighbouring ghosts of Luton and Dunstable and divided the book up into several broad sections: roads and open places, haunted houses and other buildings, public houses, with the ghostly history of St Albans Cathedral having a chapter all to itself. There is also a ghost walk taking in several of the sites covered in the text. This book, like the previous one, includes accounts and comparisons with other national hauntings and paranormal experiences which I feel are relevant to the discussions in hand, and which help to shed a greater light on this shadowy, fascinating, at times frightening, and for many, continually stimulating subject.

The great film director and screenwriter Stanley Kubrick, who admitted to a long interest in the subject of the paranormal, once called tales of ghosts and horror 'archetypes of the unconscious' that enable us to see the 'dark side' without having to confront it directly. Ghost stories also appeal to what he described as mankind's 'craving for immortality'. 'If you can be afraid of a ghost, then you have to believe that a ghost may exist. And if a ghost exists, then oblivion might not be the end.' Perhaps it is fitting that the director of the 1980 cult classic *The Shining*, based on the best-selling novel by horror maestro Stephen King, lived at Childwickbury Manor on the outskirts of St Albans for over twenty years; several of his most famous films were completed here. He died at Childwickbury in 1999, aged seventy.

In closing it is worth pointing out that where the mysterious world of the paranormal is concerned, one fact is clear: new ghosts are constantly being seen, convincing cases of haunting are always occurring and previously unreported accounts of supernormal happenings gradually come into the public domain, with the result that regional guides such as this one can never be finite or complete documents of the supernatural history of a particular town or place. I am always interested in collecting details of new experiences or additional information on any of the cases included in this survey, either for a future edition or a sequel volume – readers can contact me in confidence through my website.

As Luton-born ghost hunter Tony Broughall has commented: 'Like time and space, the ghosts seem to go on forever'.

Paul Adams
October 2013

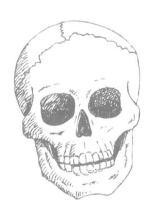

1

ROADS, HIGHWAYS AND OPEN SPACES

IN paranormal terms, the annals of organised ghost hunting and psychical research show that the roads of Britain appear to be populated by an unusually wide and at times frightening collection of apparitions and supernatural forms. Not all of these ghostly road users are phantom figures or even human in origin: there are numerous reports of phantom vehicles, animals (including numerous phantom dogs) and even birds and unidentified cryptids.

In 1961, Stanley Prescott, a motorist from Dunstable, was forced off the road by a phantom black Morris saloon while driving along the A4146 near Edlesborough, Buckinghamshire. The car, unseen by Prescott's wife, vanished as suddenly as it had appeared. The appearance of a similar vehicle, this time stationary and apparently broken down, has traditionally been the cause of minor accidents on stretches of the A41 Watford bypass in years gone by. Further afield, on the Isle of Skye in the Inner Hebrides, another phantom car – in this case a 1934 Austin – has been infrequently reported since

the 1940s. All accounts, and there are four named witnesses in the records, describe the car as travelling at great speed with headlights blazing but no driver at the wheel. During the writing of this book I was told by an AA recovery driver about the experience of his father who, while driving alone on a road in Wiltshire, was confronted by the startling appearance of a seemingly driverless car which came towards him on a collision course, before suddenly vanishing in an instant. Public vehicles have also joined the ranks of this mysterious and unquiet fleet, the most famous of which, a phantom double-decker Routemaster bus, was said to have been the cause of several accidents, one fatal, in the Ladbroke Grove area of West London during the 1930s.

There is also a number of reports, of varying quality, involving phantom cyclists. A skeletal rider who passes unsuspecting pedestrians in the roadway outside the former church of St Mary at Woodhorn in Northumberland appears to be little more than a local legend. A more convincing case involving a named witness and collected by writer Peter Moss for his book *Ghosts Over Britain*, took place in wartime Northampton in 1940 when a local man, George Dodds, encountered the apparition of a headless cyclist, apparently the victim of a pre-war traffic accident. Interestingly, our first St Albans ghost also involves a spectral cyclist – one that was seen several times by a number of people during the mid-1950s.

One autumn evening shortly after seven o'clock, St Albans resident Mary Myers was driving along Sandpit Lane on her way to nearby Hatfield. As she rounded a bend in the road near the junction with Coopers Green Lane, the rear light of a solitary cyclist came into view and Mrs Myers slowed down to overtake what she could clearly make out, despite the failing light, to be a man in shirtsleeves wearing a trilby hat and what appeared to be either a waistcoat or knitted sleeveless jumper. Passing the rider, she glanced back into her rear view mirror and was amazed to find that the figure had completely vanished. Only seconds had elapsed between her car overtaking the cyclist, making it impossible for the rider and his bicycle to have left the road on a section of the country lane where there were no immediate turn offs. Puzzled by the incident, Mary continued on her way, but her encounter with the ghostly rider was not finished. Over the next three weeks, while driving along the same stretch of road, the phantom cyclist appeared a further four times, always in the same place, suddenly coming into view and then disappearing within a matter of seconds. Mrs Myers was not the only person to experience the phenomenon, as at the time a number of letters were published in the *Herts Advertiser* from residents who also claimed to have seen the solitary rider. The origins of this haunting, which appears not to have been reported for many years, is unclear, although at the time there were reports that it may have been linked with the death of an Italian prisoner of war who was allegedly killed by a car on the same stretch of road.

The origins of road ghosts and hauntings are inevitably linked with local accidents and roadside tragedies. In the early 1900s, interest in a mysterious light phenomenon on what is now the B653 at New Mill End, 4 miles north of St Albans, also reached the correspondence column of the *Herts Advertiser*. This corpse light (known in America as a 'spook light') was at the time connected with the spot near the road where a local resident committed suicide, although its real origins remain unknown. The same section of highway is also associated with the apparitions of a ghostly horse and rider and an eerie black figure carrying a lantern, although neither appear to have been reported for many years and may in fact be local inventions based on the turn of the century ghost light incident.

Moving closer to the outskirts of St Albans, the B651 at Nomansland Common is another road with distinctly supernatural associations. In *Haunted Luton and Dunstable*, I briefly described the criminal career of the seventeenth-century female highwayman Katherine Ferrers, whose ghost is said to haunt the grounds and roads near her former home of Markyate Cell, close to the A5 trunk road south of Dunstable. Her short but dramatic life, portrayed by Margaret Lockwood in the 1945 cinema film *The Wicked Lady*, came to a sudden and violent end in 1659 at the age of

Katherine Ferrers, whose ghost is said to haunt the roads crossing Nomansland Common.

was highly distressed by the incident, and it was some time before the petrified animal could be persuaded to move away from the spot. Dogs have long been known to have psychic faculties and psychic literature contains numerous instances of their spontaneous reactions to supernormal phenomena. Douglas Payne's experience appears to be an isolated one, but The Wicked Lady public house itself is also known to be a haunted building. In *Two Haunted Counties*, Tony Broughall reports that the sounds of a woman sobbing and crying have been heard by former members of staff on a number of occasions.

The importance of St Albans in the history of Roman Britain has not surprisingly led to several alleged sightings of ghostly figures associated with this period across this part of west Hertfordshire. The countryside around the market town of Tring, described by Sheila Richards as 'The most haunted town in Hertfordshire', has several Roman ghosts: the B488 road at Bulbourne is known to be haunted by the apparitions of wounded Roman soldiers injured during skirmishes with Queen Boudicca's forces, while in July 1865, the *Buckinghamshire Advertiser* reported that a large Roman encampment was seen early in the morning on several successive days on Wiggington Common. As well as the phantom horse of Katherine Ferrers, the B651 is also known for the appearance of spectral Roman soldiers in an incident collected by Luton Paranormal Society archivist William King. According to local tradition, the sound of a column of marching men has been heard along this stretch of road, sometimes accompanied by visual apparitions of the soldiers themselves. However, actual dated sightings involving

twenty-five when she was shot and fatally wounded while attempting to rob a coach crossing Nomansland Common. As well as surviving in the naming of two local landmarks – Ferrers Lane which runs from the Wheathampstead road westwards towards Harpenden and The Wicked Lady public house on the north side of the common itself – this historic tragedy appears to have left other more eerie and inexplicable marks. In December 1970, the then manager of The Wicked Lady, Douglas Payne, was walking his dog late one evening in the vicinity of Nomansland Common when he became aware of the sound of what appeared to be a galloping horse approaching from a distance. It was a still night, around half past eleven. To the publican's amazement, the sound grew in intensity and, despite nothing being visible, passed by within touching distance before fading away into silence. Mr Payne's dog, however,

On the B651 between Wheathampstead and St Albans, a column of marching Roman soldiers has sometimes been encountered by travellers late at night.. (Recreation by Eddie Brazil)

named witnesses appear to be lacking and like many provincial hauntings, this particular one remains very much anecdotal in nature. The case is mentioned briefly by the late Betty Puttick, a former St Albans resident and author of several paranormal books. In her book *Ghosts of Hertfordshire*, she describes an incident on a November night 'not long ago' involving a group of people returning to St Albans by car from Wheathampstead. According to Puttick, the car driver witnessed the sounds and paranormal vision of a marching column of Roman legionaries with a standard bearer at their head; the passengers in the car, who like the driver are unnamed, also heard the sounds of tramping footsteps and the jingling of metal but were deprived a glimpse of the ghosts themselves.

Staying for a moment in the area north of St Albans, it is worth looking briefly at an interesting haunting that is associated with an unusual and still unsolved local murder. On the evening of Monday 30 December 1957, Anne Noblett, the seventeen-year-old daughter of a local farming family, went missing after returning home to Wheathampstead from a dancing class at nearby Harpenden. She was last seen getting off a bus outside the Cherry Tree pub on the Lower Luton Lane and starting the quarter of a mile walk up Marshalls Heath Lane to her parent's isolated farmhouse. A month later, her fully-clothed body was discovered by an RAF serviceman and his brother walking their dog in woods on the outskirts of Whitwell village. The case achieved notoriety at the time due to the suggestion by celebrated Home Office pathologist Francis Camps that the remarkable lack of decomposition of the body was due to the fact that it had been stored for some length of time at an extremely low temperature, most likely in a refrigerator; but despite much publicity and police work, the 'Deep Freeze Murder' was never solved and the killer of Anne Noblett ultimately escaped justice.

In early January 1975, the *Herts Advertiser* reported that in the preceding months, workers at industrial premises in Marshalls Heath Lane adjacent to the former Noblett farm had had a number of unnerving encounters with what they believed to be the ghost of the murdered farmer's daughter. The phenomena, which took place regularly throughout the autumn and early winter of 1974 before gradually petering out, comprised incidents of a poltergeist nature including psychic touches, the opening and closing of doors and the appearance of a mysterious female figure. Staff at the plant hire company became unhappy about working in certain areas alone and two employees eventually refused to stay there after dark.

Bob Shambrook, a twenty-four-year-old workman from Ware, was alone one night when a stable door adjacent to the company building began opening and shutting by itself. Disturbed by the noise, Shambrook fastened the latch securely on three occasions, but each time the door seemingly opened unaided and repeatedly banged against the wall. There was no wind and Shambrook was certain no one could have played a trick on him without being seen. Another employee, Alfred Spink, a mechanic in his mid-forties from nearby Harpenden,

Anne Noblett: her 'Deep Freeze Murder' in 1957 remains unsolved. (Paul Heslop)

also reported strange experiences. Alone in one of the outbuildings one evening, he was feeding a local cat when he had the unmistakable impression of something brushing against the side of his head. Immediately turning round, he saw he was quite alone but the experience was both convincing and unsettling. Another worker at the farm also reported the same cat hissing and arching its back at an apparently empty space on several occasions. Similar happenings continued at Marshalls Heath Lane for several weeks, almost as though they were building up to what became the most notable phenomenon associated with the haunting.

One evening a workman noticed a young girl standing by a single-storey storage shed near to one of the old farm outbuildings. Assuming it was a local child playing about, he shouted across and walked towards her, but by the time

The derelict farm buildings at Marshalls Heath Lane, Wheathampstead, where strange happenings took place during the autumn and winter of 1974. (Paul Adams)

he reached the spot, the figure had disappeared. Like his colleagues he was convinced that no one could have hidden in the vicinity of the outbuildings without being seen, or likewise have passed by him unnoticed. The shed itself was locked, as was the barn immediately adjacent, the only other building in the immediate vicinity. The workman was not close enough to describe the face of the figure in any detail but Alf Spink, convinced by his own experiences that something genuinely paranormal was taking place, was also certain that the ghost of the tragic Anne Noblett was in fact haunting the old farm. Back in 1957, Spink, then aged twenty-four, had joined hundreds of volunteers in searching the surrounding countryside for the missing teenager.

Today the buildings in Marshalls Heath Lane where this unusual haunting took place lie empty and unused and the ghost of Anne Noblett, if it was in fact the young murder victim, has not been seen for many years. When I examined the case while researching for a survey of British crime with paranormal connections (*Ghosts & Gallows*), I was told by the present owners that in the early 2000s, a séance held in the derelict outbuildings by a group of Hertfordshire spiritualists had made contact with the spirit of the murdered Anne Noblett, who named her killer as a man who at the time was alive and living at nearby Whipsnade in Bedfordshire. Despite this revelation, both the criminal and paranormal aspects of the case remain unsolved.

From twentieth-century crime, we cross the years to briefly look at a colourful local legend that has an interesting connection with one of the most

A contemporary illustration of Witchfinder General, Matthew Hopkins, interrogating a suspect. Hopkins passed through St Albans in the mid-1600s.

sinister and violent periods of English history. The streets of St Albans have traditionally been the haunt of a sinister witch-like apparition known as Mother Haggy, who has her origins in a satirical ghost story that first appeared in pamphlet form at the beginning of the eighteenth century. In *The Story of St. Alb-n's Ghost or the Apparition of Mother Haggy collected from the best manuscripts*, the eponymous spectre of the title is described as living at the time of James I when, as the wife of a local yeoman, was a much liked and respected member of the community. However, she later turned to evil and became a black witch, and as such subjected the citizens for several years to a campaign of fear and intimidation using magical powers and devilry. After her death, the good people of St Albans breathed a sigh of relief, but their happiness was short-lived as her unquiet ghost was soon seen in many parts of the town. As well as the streets and buildings, the frightening apparition of Mother Haggy, sometimes appearing in human form, at other times as a cat, a hen and even a lion, was known to roam the surrounding woods and fields at night on a broomstick. She is said to have crossed from one bank of the River Ver to the other supported by a kettledrum, like an English version of the classic Russian folktale of Baba Jaga.

Although Mother Haggy may be imaginary, the spectre of witchcraft in seventeenth century St Albans was a real one. In 1649, during the time of the notorious witch trials that raged across neighbouring Essex and Suffolk, Elizabeth Knott and John Palmer were tried and hanged as witches; two people out of a dozen who were put on trial in the county the same year. A short time before, one of the most notorious figures in the history of English witchcraft, the self-styled Witchfinder General, Matthew Hopkins, passed briefly through the town on his way north to Bedford. Hopkins, immortalised by horror actor Vincent Price in director Michael Reeves' 1968 film *Witchfinder General*, as well as several modern biographies and even in heavy metal music, was a young opportunist who seized on the climate of superstitious fear rife in the country during the time of the Civil War. He carved out a career for himself and his associate John Stearne by travelling the east of England investigating cases of alleged witchcraft and sorcery. The two men claimed to have been appointed by Parliament (but in fact held no official position) and in a two-year period beginning in 1645 were responsible for the trial and execution of over 300 women. Hopkins retired from the profession in 1647 and quickly published his own manual of witch-hunting techniques entitled *The Discovery of Witches*, but died the same year, most likely of tuberclulosis, at his home in Manningtree, Essex, aged twenty-seven. Details of his early life are scant however, so he may even have been as young as twenty-five.

The English Civil War is a period of St Albans' history to which we will return later in our survey. Ghostly sounds connected with an earlier period of internal violence in the country form another anecdotal road haunting, this time involving Holywell Hill, a main thoroughfare that crosses the River Ver to the south of the city centre, and where houses are known to have existed from the middle of the twelfth century. Here, ghost hunter Tony Broughall has reported the supernatural noises of armed conflict being heard on occasion, although specific accounts are lacking. The sound of horses' hooves, shouted commands and the ring of steel are thought to be a psychic replay (and possibly a cyclical haunting) of parts of the First Battle of St Albans which took place in 1455 and ushered in what is now famously described as the War of the Roses. On 22 May of that year, King Henry VI along with a Lancastrian force of around 2,000 men commanded by Edmund, Duke of Somerset, occupied southerly sections of the town including the area around Sopwell Lane, as well as the central market square. A larger Yorkist army under Richard Plantagenet, 3rd Duke of York, together with his ally Richard Neville, the 16th Earl of Warwick, were camped a short distance away on open farmland to the east. For several hours, protracted negotiations between the two groups took place. When these broke down, the Duke of York led two assaults against the Lancastrian lines but was beaten back on both occasions with the loss of many of his troops. However, while fighting raged on the southern side of the town, Richard Neville took a small group of men and made his way to the market square where, with the element of surprise, he was able to outflank and attack the Duke of Somerset's men. Edmund the Duke, together with two of his supporters, Henry Percy, 2nd Earl of Northumberland and Thomas Clifford, High Sheriff of Westmorland, were killed while King Henry was injured by arrow fire and subsequently captured, after which the defeated Lancastrians abandoned the town.

Another local conflict, again a campaign of the War of the Roses, which has become known as the Second Battle of St Albans, took place on Shrove Tuesday, 17 February 1461, when a Lancastrian army of over 15,000 soldiers led by a youthful trio of noblemen that included Henry Percy, 3rd Earl of Northumberland and John Clifford, 9th Baron de Clifford (known as 'The Butcher' due to his execution of Edmund, Earl of Rutland following the Battle of Wakefield the previous year), were intercepted as they marched on London by a rival Yorkist force again commanded by Richard Neville, the 16th Earl of Warwick. The Lancastrians attacked St Albans in a dawn raid but were driven back from the town centre by concentrated arrow-fire from Neville's archers. A second assault was successful, however, and having gained the town, the Lancastrians began to engage Neville's rear guard which was camped out in woodland at Bernards Heath a mile away to the north (where nowadays the A1081 road runs northwards towards Harpenden). Here the damp winter weather affected the Yorkist powder magazines and with limited cannon and musket fire, coupled with tactical problems in moving soldiers out of the besieged town, Neville realised the engagement was lost and retreated with his remaining company of around 4,000 men to the relative safety of Chipping Norton in Oxfordshire.

Today the area around Bernards Heath is occupied by modern housing. It is difficult to imagine the grim scenes of warfare that were played out here over 500 years ago. However, one St Albans resident who claimed to have stepped back momentarily to that violent and bloody day was the

The haunted woods at Bernards Heath, where writer Betty Puttick saw the time-slip ghost of a fifteenth-century soldier. (Eddie Brazil)

aforementioned Betty Puttick, formerly of Waverley Road, a leading light of the Verulam Writers' Circle. Puttick was the author of a number of regional paranormal books across the Chilterns and beyond, and we will encounter her again later in this book in connection with the haunting of the great abbey church. In *Ghosts of Hertfordshire*, Puttick describes an incident that happened during the daytime while walking her dog across Bernards Heath. Suddenly and without warning, she seemed to be surrounded by the sounds and movements of a vast and invisible conflict, as soldiers and riders threw themselves together in a desperate battle for survival: neighing horses, shouted commands, and the clash

of swords, accompanied by the violent movement of unseen bodies quickly blocked out the ordinary everyday sounds and atmosphere of the normally calm woodland scene. Unsettled by the frightening experience, she raised her arms over her head and turned to walk back the way she had come. It was at this point that the writer and ghost hunter saw the apparition of what she took to be an injured soldier sitting with his back to a tree: 'He was wearing a leather cap and jerkin, boots and some sort of leggings and he had a bow and arrows. He was holding his head in his hands and I could tell he was wounded and in pain.' As she continued to look, the vision began to fade, and moments later the

Haunted Woods.

figure had vanished – with it went the strange and alarming sensations of supernatural conflict. Collecting her dog, Puttick emerged from the trees back into the ordinary twentieth-century scene of cars, overhead aeroplanes and modern buildings. There was now no sign of the ghostly battle.

This strange 'time-slip'-type haunting is not without precedent, and there are a number of examples of similar happenings around the country. Puttick's experience brings to mind the haunted church of St Lawrence at Alton in Hampshire, where several people, including the Hampshire historian Dorothea St Hill Bourne, have encountered the sensation of invisible fighting inside the building, seemingly a psychic imprint of an event that took place during the English Civil War: the Royalist Colonel Boles' desperate last stand attempt against Sir William Waller and his Cromwellian troops. The change in the atmosphere – Puttick later described an unnatural silence with the trees becoming 'completely still, with no movement in the leaves' so that the whole scene resembled 'a painted backdrop' – is a common feature of this form of intriguing paranormal experience, but despite many recorded examples, the phenomenon currently remains unexplained. Another local example from Stockwood Park in neighbouring Bedfordshire is included in my book *Haunted Luton and Dunstable*.

Holywell Hill, St Albans, at the beginning of the twentieth century, where the ghost of a Victorian woman was seen walking in the late 1980s.

Such explosions of human violence as played out during the Battles of St Albans, despite the passage of over 500 years, may well have imprinted themselves in some (presently) unknowable way in the land and surroundings around the scene of the bloodiest of the fighting; there are a number of former battlefield sites across the country that have similar ghostly associations. In his book *Hauntings and Apparitions*, published to mark the centenary of the Society for Psychical Research in 1982, Andrew Mackenzie records the experience of a female witness who seemingly encountered a psychic replay of the aftermath of the Battle of Nechtansmere, which took place between the Picts and the Northumbrians near the village of Dunnichen in Angus in May 685.

The paranormal vision, which lasted for some time, involved the appearance of corpse lights as well as phantom figures of living womenfolk attending the prone bodies of the dead and dying. Other former battlefield sites with ghostly associations include Braddock Down, near Lostwithiel in Cornwall, scene of a Royalist victory during the Civil War on 19 January 1643, and Cheriton, near Alresford in Hampshire, where Parliamentarian forces under Sir William Waller fought and defeated an opposing army led by Sir Ralph Hopton. Perhaps the most interesting British battlefield haunting, and one of the best examples of the stone tape explanation in this context, is that of Edgehill in Warwickshire. A month after Prince Rupert had commanded a 15,000-strong

Verulamium Park, known for the ghosts of a Roman soldier and a Civil War Cavalier who appears in a haze of silver light. (Eddie Brazil)

army against an equally large force under the Earl of Essex on 23 October 1642, shepherds and local people reported seeing visions of soldiers again locked in combat, accompanied by the supernatural sounds of cannon and musket fire. On Christmas Eve of the same year, the Edgehill ghosts returned and a group of investigating officers instructed by Charles II to make enquiries into the happenings confirmed that they had seen the phantom re-enactment for themselves. Interestingly, they claimed to have recognised the apparition of Prince Rupert, the king's nephew, who at the time was still alive; a ghost of the living, who like the other components of the 'haunting', had become somehow imprinted in the atmosphere of this particular section of countryside where over a thousand men lost their lives in a single afternoon.

Another haunting from Holywell Hill, less dramatic than the sounds of a phantom battle but equally as fascinating, has been collected by Hertfordshire-based ghost hunter and writer Damien O'Dell. In *Paranormal Hertfordshire*, O'Dell describes the experiences of a correspondent, Martin Oliver, who in the late 1980s was an employee of Fernau Avionics, a designer and manufacturer of navigational equipment for civil and military aircraft. At the time they were based in premises close to the River Ver at the southern end of Holywell Hill, a site now occupied by the Latium Close development. During a lunch break, Oliver was making his way up Holywell Hill when, at the junction with Belmont Hill,

Part of the original town wall of Roman Verulamium. (Eddie Brazil)

he became aware of a woman walking in the same direction along the pavement in front of him. The manner of her dress made her instantly conspicuous, as she seemed to have stepped out from another century: the woman was dressed in a woollen shawl over a wide ankle-length skirt, wore brown leather boots and a cloth hat with a wide brim, and was carrying a wicker basket on her left arm, in the manner of a flower seller. Unable to pass the woman on the narrow pavement, Oliver waited for a break in the traffic coming towards him, then stepped out into the road and quickly overtook the eccentric-looking pedestrian. As he glanced back out of curiosity to see what the woman looked like, he was astonished to see that the

figure had completely disappeared and that the entire stretch of pavement down Holywell Hill on that side of the road was empty. Of the strange Victorian-looking lady there was no sign ...

Verulamium Park is a landscaped open space of over 100 acres located on the south-west side of the city, close to the grounds of the abbey church. Here parts of the old city walls from the time of the Roman occupation can be seen, as well as the ornamental lake that lies parallel to the course of the River Ver. The river, which flows through the park, was created in the 1930s by unemployed workmen from Wales and the north of England following archaeological excavations carried out by Mortimer Wheeler. Not surprisingly, the ghost of a Roman soldier is associated with the site but it appears to be a relatively recently reported phenomenon, limited to one account dating from 1985 when on a summer's evening, an unnamed witness in his mid-20s reported seeing the apparition of a Roman centurion on horseback. This particular haunting was first included by Muriel Thresher and Beryl Carrington of the St Albans and Hertfordshire Architectural and Archaeological Society, in their 1987 pamphlet 'St Albans Ghost Lore', and has since been included in the writings of other commentators. Fifteen years before, around Christmas time 1970, another phantom figure, this time the arresting figure of a Civil War Cavalier complete with sword, is said to have appeared one evening to two young cyclists in a haze of silver light. Thresher and Carrington also report the appearance of other Roman apparitions in nearby King Harry Lane, but details of this particular haunting are lacking.

One long-time St Albans resident who claimed to have had a number of supernatural encounters in Verulamium Park was the colourful John Mills, best known to many people as Ginger Mills. Originally from London and Pershore in Worcestershire, Mills – a former circus performer – arrived in St Albans in the late 1960s and for many years lived out of a camper van parked in various locations around the city. On one occasion, during the early hours of the morning and while walking around the ornamental lake, Mills claimed to have heard the sound of marching feet and experienced a cold breeze as a phantom army of invisible Roman soldiers moved past him in the darkness. Whatever happened that night will now never be known for certain as Ginger Mills died in the Worcestershire Royal Infirmary in February 2008, taking the secrets of the Verulamium ghosts with him.

Leaving aside the Marshalls Heath Lane haunting and the legendary adventures of Mother Haggy, the remaining phenomena that we have looked at so far could all reasonably be explained away using the principle of the atmospheric photograph or stone tape ghost. The phantom cyclist, marching soldiers, as well as the sounds of galloping horses (whether ridden by the ghostly Katherine Ferrers or not) give the impression of being spontaneous replays of past events that in some unknown way manifest themselves in the vision and hearing of unsuspecting witnesses who happen to have been in the right place at the right time to act as living receivers for these bizarre broadcasts from the past. Although the principle of the stone tape has a believable logic of its own, how such a phenomenon could actually work is at present beyond understanding, although in recent years the mysterious world of quantum physics has appeared to some to be the place where some of the answers may lie. Quantum mechanics, the study of the world inside the atom, where the activities of sub-atomic particles are shrouded in uncertainty and the actual process of observation appears to change the behaviour of the things being observed, seems at first glance to have a natural affinity with the world of the paranormal. In his book *The Roots of Coincidence*, the Hungarian-British writer and psychical researcher Arthur Koestler suggested that the activities of the ghost-like neutrino particle, first discovered in 1956, showed that science at last had an explanation for the countless reports of apparitions and phantom figures walking through solid walls: it has been postulated that a neutrino would stand a good chance of passing through a thickness of lead stretching to the nearest star without actually hitting anything.

However, the reality of quantum science is that, despite its seemingly inherent mystery, it is possible to predict the results of quantum experiments with astonishing accuracy – the evolutionary biologist Richard Dawkins cites an analogy of correctly calculating the width of North America to the accuracy of the width of a single human hair – and despite the appeal to both psychical researchers and New Age practitioners alike, it seems likely that the actual physics of the paranormal is a bizarre and perhaps ultimately unknowable combination (or interaction) of natural science, chemistry and human psychology.

For the next part of our St Albans ghost hunt, we leave the misty haunted byways and head for the travellers' rest to explore a selection of the city's most interesting and haunted pubs and hostelries.

2

HAUNTED PUBLIC HOUSES AND HOSTELRIES

HOTELS, public houses and inns are known as some of the most persistently haunted buildings in Britain. Guy Lyon Playfair, writer and investigator of the famous Enfield poltergeist case in the late 1970s, listed several hundred individual haunted pubs in a survey carried out in the mid-1980s, and today most counties have their own dedicated paranormal guides covering this particular facet of the haunted landscape. St Albans has over the years been home to dozens of drinking houses and hostelries, and here we look briefly at the haunted histories of a number of the most notable and interesting establishments.

Situated in Abbey Mill Lane on the edge of the haunted Verulamium Park, Ye Olde Fighting Cocks is not only the most ancient hostelry in St Albans, but also vies for the title of the oldest public house in England, and is currently listed as such in the *Guinness Book of Records*. Its status in St Albans was challenged in 1994 when the remains of a Roman brewing oven were uncovered during

building work being carried out at the Black Lion Hotel in Fishpool Street, but to date its historical reputation in the city still stands. An eleventh-century building on foundations which go back to around AD 790, the pub's sixteenth-century appearance belies its age, and its unusual octagonal shape was no doubt the origin of its original name The Round House, which was changed to the current title in the 1800s. Its presence close to both the majestic Abbey Church and on stonework forming part of one of the original monastery buildings suggests that the Fighting Cocks may have a haunted history with religious associations, and it is true that the apparitions of men dressed in brown monk-like habits have been seen here. However, this is not as long-established a haunting as one would expect from the oldest public house in St Albans, and in fact dates from 2001, when a member of the bar staff claimed to have seen a procession of robed figures emerge from the ancient cellar and cross to one of the fireside tables,

Ye Olde Fighting Cocks in Abbey Mill Lane, the oldest public house in St Albans. A procession of ghostly monks was seen here in 2001. (Eddie Brazil)

where they seated themselves before fading away. This experience took place around half past nine one morning, and the witness stated that the ghostly figures were only visible from the knee up. The movement of objects is another phenomenon reported to occur here on occasion.

The distinctive oversailing upper storey of the fifteenth-century galleried Goat Inn in Sopwell Lane makes up one of the pleasant street scenes on the south side of the city. Originally built as a private house, its position on the stage-coach route from London was exploited in the late 1780s when it was converted into an inn. By the late 1700s it was highly regarded for its local ale as well as the extensive stabling provided for changes of coach horse – over seventy animals could be accommodated at any one time as opposed to less than a dozen human guests. Two hundred years later, beginning in the early 1920s, The Goat became a lodging house often used by navvies and road workers before eventually changing back to the public house which residents and visitors continue to enjoy today. Given this interesting history, it should come as no surprise that The Goat Inn has a reputation as a haunted building that goes back many years. Here an unusual atmosphere over and above what one would normally expect to feel in an old house or building has been commented on by many visitors. A correspondent, James, who contacted me through the

The Goat Inn, Sopwell Lane. The strange movement of objects and apparitions were reported here in the late 1970s, but reports of a strange atmosphere on the premises go back many years. (Eddie Brazil)

Herts Advertiser, knew The Goat Inn when he was young man. His grandmother worked there as a cleaner, and described a brooding feeling of being constantly watched while present inside. In the late 1970s, Peter Ransom became the licensee, staying for eight years, and Damien O'Dell has collected accounts of a number of his experiences while living and working on the premises. These include a door opening and closing by itself, the mysterious movement of objects including an acoustic guitar which was found several times in a totally different place from where Ransom had left it, and the appearance of an apparition with a 'ghastly face' which the landlord woke up one night to see standing at the foot of his bed, accompanied by an intense and unnatural drop in temperature which filled the entire room. A short walk down Sopwell Lane is The White Lion, an attractive sixteenth-century hostelry that, like The Goat, operated for many years as a coaching inn. Here both staff and customers have claimed to have seen the partial apparition of a young woman. The bar area and a flight of stairs leading down into the beer cellar appear to be the most haunted areas, but a number of sightings lack both dates and named witnesses. As such, the haunting remains somewhat unsatisfactory.

A direct contrast to these and a number of other old St Albans hostelries with paranormal associations is the case of a more modern establishment,

The former Tudor Tavern, which has since been converted into a restaurant. Accounts of a haunting, including a shadowy figure following members of staff, date back to the 1960s. (Eddie Brazil)

the King William IV, a 1930s road pub located to the north-east of the city centre on a prominent corner site opposite the junction of Sandridge Road and Marshalswick Lane. Built in 1937 and today operated by the Ember Inns chain, the King William quickly established itself in the local area as a haunted building when staff talked about seeing an unidentified figure in the bar area, and glasses were reported to have been thrown about and broken. This particular haunting has a distinct military flavour, perhaps because the pub was used by a local division of the Home Guard as a drill hall soon after it was built – the apparition of a soldier wearing a moustache and dressed in uniform has been reported here a number of times. He was seen by two witnesses in 1987, the head chef and the landlord, who both described a tall man wearing a green-coloured uniform: this was a collective sighting, as summoned by a shout from the cellar, the landlord arrived in time to see the figure clearly before it faded away moments later. To date this appears to be the last sighting of this particular ghost.

Returning to the centre of St Albans as well as stepping back in time several centuries, we can briefly examine the haunted history of an early fifteenth-century building that for many years was known as the Tudor Tavern, but at the time of writing has been converted into the Thai Square restaurant, situated on the corner of Verulam Road and

George Street, a short distance from the imposing Abbey Church. George Street is an ancient thoroughfare and was at first known as Churchstreet, a name that first appears in recorded history in 1245. At one time the north side of the street boasted a complex of several inns and hostelries including The White Horse, The Bear (also known as The Bull), The Tabard (which later became the Antelope) and The Valiant Trooper, which also went by the name of The White Bear. Originally known as The Swan, the old Tudor Tavern was an amalgamation of two medieval hostelries, the Swan and the George, and in the mid-1450s was part of Sopwell Priory, an Abbey cell that we will briefly encounter in the next chapter – in the cellar of the building, a tunnel is known to exist that runs across the road in the direction of the abbey itself. Originally an unheated chamber, a chimney stack and fireplaces were added in the sixteenth century, and following the Restoration in 1660, the hostelry became known as The King's Head. By 1790, it had ceased operating as a public house and had become divided into two private dwellings. Later, shop premises were opened on the ground floor and the former King's Head was for some time a candle factory. In the early 1900s the building was divided into the Mayles antique shop and a photographic portrait studio; a surgical supplies business also operated from the address at this time. In the early 1960s, the building was purchased by St Albans Council and subsequently refurbished and re-opened as a public house, The Tudor Tavern.

It would seem that such a wealth of history and human activity may in some way have become imprinted in the old walls, beams and timbers of the historic crown-post roof structure of this ancient building, as over the years, staff members and owners have told a number of stories of ghostly encounters here. A shadowy figure has been perhaps the most frequently reported phenomenon, apparently following staff about as they have cleaned up the bar area after closing time. The apparition's identity is unknown, although there have been several suggestions, ranging from a former landlord to a casualty from the First Battle of St Albans. As well as the 'shadow', a more substantial but equally unidentifiable apparition has been reported from the Tudor Tavern, namely a dark-haired, bearded man wearing a ruffed Elizabethan-style costume who appeared briefly seated at a table, drinking a glass of ale witnessed by a manager, a psychic imprint that befits a building with such history. Poltergeist-type activity, including the movement of objects and interference with electrical equipment and light switches, a common phenomenon in haunted premises, has also been reported here over the years. This type of allegedly paranormal activity has also been reported from another old pub building close to the Tudor Tavern, although The Boot Inn is a comparative youngster – its record as a licensed premises dates from 1719, although buildings are known to have occupied the site from the beginning of the 1500s and this particular plot has undergone much physical change over the centuries. In the late 1890s, the public house shared part of the ground floor with a tobacconists and a barber's shop, and it was not until

The Boot Inn: the paranormal interference with electrical equipment, a common feature of many hauntings, has been experienced here. (Paul Adams)

the early 1960s that The Boot was finally enlarged into the premises that it comprises today. The switching on and off of fruit machines and a juke box, as well as overhead lighting, has been reported here in recent years, although unlike the Tudor Tavern, there appear to be no records of apparitions being seen.

Our final port of call on this brief pub tour of haunted St Albans is at one of the city's most attractive buildings, the sixteenth-century White Hart Hotel, the oldest sections of which date back to around 1500. Originally called

the Hartshorn, the White Hart was one of over a dozen inns that at one time (the late 1500s-early 1600s) formed an almost unbroken line of taverns and hostelries on the east side of Holywell Hill, from the Cross Keys at the junction with London Road to the north, down to The Horsehead at the south, just past the intersection with Sopwell Lane. In 1746, Simon Fraser, 11th Lord Lovat, the Jacobite rebel who was one of many Highlanders defeated at the Battle of Culloden, stayed a night at the White Hart on his way to the Tower of London. Lovat had the distinction of

The attractive White Hart on Holywell Hill, where poltergeist activity and the appearance of phantom figures have been recorded. (Paul Adams)

being the last man to be beheaded in England when he mounted the scaffold on Tower Green on 19 March 1747. By the early 1800s, over seventy mail coaches were passing daily through St Albans carrying up to 600 passengers. In 1820, as the Northampton coach turned off Holywell Hill and passed under the archway leading to the stable yard at the rear of the building, Elizabeth Wilson, who was riding on the roof, failed to duck her head and was struck and fatally injured. There is a possibility that she may be one of several ghosts that have been both seen and felt in this old coaching inn over the years, and may be the figure of a woman encountered on a number of occasions by both staff and guests. The death of Elizabeth Wilson is said to be the inspiration for the death of Mrs Jingle in Charles Dickens' 1836 novel *The Pickwick Papers*. Another female apparition at the White Hart is that of a small girl, seen standing by the fireplace in the main bar room as well as in an upstairs room. A former cellar man, Jon Wollard, claimed that heavy beer barrels would often move by themselves during the night hours.

As with a number of haunted buildings in our survey, there are also reports of doors opening and closing by themselves and room lights turning on and off. Perhaps the most bizarre phenomenon said to have taken place at the White Hart is the appearance of phantom writing on a dressing-table mirror in one of the guest bedrooms. This is the same room where towels and other objects have been found thrown about – room number eight, for those

The galleried entrance to the White Hart, scene of a fatal coaching accident in 1820. (Paul Adams)

Simon Fraser, 11th Lord Lovat, the last person to suffer execution by beheading in England. Lovat stayed a night at the White Hart in St Albans on his way to the Tower in 1746.

who may be tempted to stay a night here to experience the happenings for themselves. Cold breezes and the sensation of an invisible presence have also been reported by staff members here on several occasions. A number of other hostelries with paranormal associations are covered briefly in a later section of the book. The next part of our survey comprises an examination of the city's most notable building, the impressive Cathedral and Abbey Church of St Alban.

3

GHOSTS OF THE ABBEY CHURCH

OF all the buildings that can provide a suitable background medium for storing psychic images and information, simply by their sheer age as well as the human history associated with their founding and use, the churches and abbeys of England must rank, along with castles and other fortified buildings, as being perhaps the most suitable. Their history stretches back in many cases for nearly a thousand years. Many of our ecclesiastical and religious buildings have ghostly associations, and churchyards and cemeteries are potent symbols of the strange and at times entertaining world of the paranormal. One twentieth-century ghost hunter, who like Tom Lethbridge considered ghosts and hauntings in purely scientific terms, was Benson Herbert, an Oxford graduate who spent many years in an enthusiastic and unorthodox investigation of the paranormal. Today a somewhat neglected figure, Herbert, who died in 1991 at the age of seventy-seven, originated a branch of paranormal enquiry that he termed

'paraphysics' and established a research organisation for its development, the Paraphysical Laboratory or 'Paralab', in an isolated farmhouse on the edge of the New Forest near Downton in Wiltshire. Herbert theorised that the massive walls of haunted castles and other similar masonry structures, such as churches and stone buildings, performed like ancient 'Faraday cages', providing a shield from external radio waves and electromagnetism, and that ghosts and apparitions were due to anomalous electrical activity trapped inside. Such a line of thinking, an alternative version of the stone tape theory that we have been considering throughout this book so far, is another non-survivalist explanation for the appearance and experience of ghostly figures and sounds within historical buildings, of which our abbeys and cathedrals are a prime example in terms of psychic and paranormal research.

The impressive outline of the Cathedral and Abbey Church of St Alban, a Grade I listed building of national

St Alban, martyred by the Romans at the end of the third century AD.

and stalled the Emperor's men for enough time to allow the preacher to escape. For Alban it was a heroic decision that was ultimately to cost him his life: refusing to both reveal the fugitive's whereabouts and recognise the regular Roman gods, Alban was summarily sentenced to death for apostasy, taken outside of the city walls and beheaded.

In the years following Alban's death, the story of his martyrdom grew and was much embellished by later writers and commentators, with tales of miraculous happenings appended to the saint's last days on earth. By the eighth century AD, when the Christian chronicler Bede was writing ghoulish descriptions of the executioner's eyes falling from his head as he swung the sword down on Alban's exposed neck as well as the River Ver parting to allow him passage to the gallows, a shrine had already been established locally, which quickly gathered a reputation as a centre for healing and pilgrimage. In time this became a Benedictine monastery and between 1077 and 1088, a Norman church was constructed. Today only the transepts, the crossing tower and the North wall of the nave remain, although the transept windows were to see a programme of late Victorian alteration by Edmund Beckett, the 1st Baron Grimthorpe, an horologist and ecclesiastical architect who in 1851 designed the clock mechanism for the chimes of Big Ben at the Palace of Westminster. Beckett carried out the work at St Albans Cathedral at his own expense, but at the time his restoration work was considered unsympathetic to the building's character.

Following the Dissolution of the Monasteries by Henry VIII in 1539,

importance, dominates the city skyline for many miles around and is visible to the traveller on practically all approaches to St Albans by road and rail. This is the oldest site of continuous Christian worship in the country, with a history that stretches back over 1,700 years. Towards the end of the third century AD during the Roman occupation of the city, a Christian priest, subsequently known as Amphibalus, was given shelter by a Romano-British citizen named Alban who was captivated enough by his visitor's preaching to convert to Christianity. According to traditional accounts, when Roman soldiers eventually arrived at Alban's villa to arrest the itinerant priest, Alban exchanged clothes with his guest the medieval Chapter House attached to the monastery site was demolished and over the next 200 years the area was looted by grave robbers intent on plundering artefacts from the site. Nearer to our own times, a new Chapter House was built in 1982 on the same spot as its predecessor and subsequently opened by Queen Elizabeth II. Over 100 years earlier, in 1877, the Abbey church had become the cathedral for the counties of Hertfordshire and Essex with the elderly Bishop of Rochester, Thomas Legh Claughton, being appointed as the first Bishop of St Albans. Claughton died in 1892 and is buried in the churchyard along with many of the former abbots, several noblemen killed in the First Battle of St Albans including Henry Percy and Edmund Beaufort, as well as the aforementioned Edmund Beckett and Robert Runcie, a former Bishop of St Albans and later Archbishop of Canterbury throughout the 1980s.

When considering the presence of the abbey's ancient stones whose columns, walls and arched ceilings have enclosed the same vaulted spaces for the passage of so many years, it is easy to follow psychical researchers like Benson Herbert and Tom Lethbridge's thinking that the building's fabric both absorbs and contains the sights, sounds and images of the past, as well as generating the conditions through which paranormal phenomena can manifest. Many of our British cathedrals have paranormal associations and in fact rank as some of the most persistently haunted buildings on record. In Newcastle-upon-Tyne, the Cathedral Church of St Nicholas is said to be haunted by the apparition of an unnamed knight dressed in full armour, whose footsteps have been heard on occasion, echoing around the building's vast interior. York Minster, in Britain's most haunted city, has a reputation for having several ghostly inhabitants: the apparition of Dean Gayle, who died in 1702 and is buried inside the cathedral, has repeatedly been seen sitting in one of the choir stalls, while on one occasion the phantom of a stonemason wearing a long apron and carrying mason's tools was reputedly seen and conversed with by a visitor. The Minster was also the setting for the appearance of a 'crisis ghost' when the apparition of a naval officer wearing full dress uniform was seen by his sister who was visiting York at the time with a party of sightseers from London. Much further south, in the City of London, the Kitchener Memorial Chapel in St Paul's Cathedral was reputedly haunted by the whistling ghost of a former official; at one time this was regarded as one of London's most well-known hauntings. Further along the Thames, Westminster Abbey has a number of varied and interesting ghosts including a haunted clock, a procession of black-clad robed figures said to have been seen one night by a policeman on duty, a monk-like figure known as 'Father Benedictus', and perhaps the abbey's most famous spectral visitor, the apparition of a khaki-clad First World War soldier, seen on occasion in the vicinity of the tomb of the Unknown Warrior. Ghosts also infest and enliven the history of many of our other notable abbeys including Whitby on the North Yorkshire coast, famous as the landing ground of Bram Stoker's literary anti-hero Dracula, and Netley on the shore of Southampton Water.

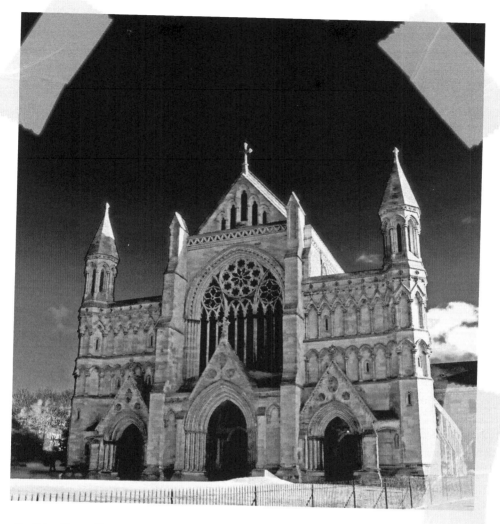

The Abbey Church of St Alban, long associated with the ghosts of singing monks. (Eddie Brazil)

For those readers interested in exploring in detail the many haunted ecclesiastical buildings of Britain, Marc Alexander's *Haunted Churches and Abbeys of Britain* and Graham McEwan's *Haunted Churches of England*, are good starting points, as well as my own *Shadows in the Nave*.

Luton-born ghost hunter Tony Broughall was one of the first researchers to set down for posterity a record of the haunting of the Cathedral and Abbey Church of St Alban, but the most complete account in recent years has been given by Betty Puttick. As the most famous report of the haunting of the Abbey Church is now fast passing from living memory, I am indebted to her compilation *Supernatural England* on which the following account is based.

Basil Saville, a sixteen-year-old former chorister, is credited as having one of the most memorable encounters with the ghosts of the city's famous cathedral, which took place during the winter of 1944 in the last months of the Second World War. Saville, a recent school leaver, was one of a regular rota of fire-watchers who spent the dark hours in and around the ancient building guarding against the dangers of incendiaries from night-time German air raids. Although St Albans escaped much of the devastation inflicted on nearby London, the abbey was a prominent local landmark and photographs of the building were issued to Luftwaffe bomber crews together with maps and half-tone aerial photographs of the area to assist with navigation during bombing raids across the northern Home Counties. On the night of 24 December 1944, Christmas Eve, the teenage youth arrived outside the abbey and let himself in through one of the side doors, expecting to find other members of the regular fire-watching party already inside. However, on this occasion Saville found the imposing Normal cathedral empty and after waiting around for some time came to the eventual and somewhat daunting conclusion that he was to spend this particular night watch on his own, the first time this had happened during all the time he had spent watching over the great building in the preceding months. There was to be no air raid on that particular night, but the young Basil Saville was to have an experience that he would never forget nonetheless.

With the surrounding wartime blackout in force and the moon just under three-quarters full, the abbey church was in darkness, with only a faint silvery glow filtering into the great vaulted interior from outside. Despite this, the teenager's familiarity with the building allowed him to move around inside with ease and he spent some time following his usual route, checking on the various items of fire-fighting equipment as he went. The routine inspection continued uneventfully despite the darkness and Saville soon found himself approaching the Saint's Chapel with its shrine to the martyr Alban, together with the watching chamber where in the 1400s the abbey monks would view the visitors as they made their pilgrimage to the holy shrine. Here the young man was suddenly overcome with the disconcerting sensation of being watched, something that previously he had never experienced inside the cathedral, although in haunted houses and other buildings it is one of the commoner aspects of reported paranormal experiences, particularly amongst psychic or supernormally sensitive people. Flashing his torch around, Saville was momentarily startled to see what he initially took to be the outlines of two hooded figures further on inside the cathedral building but quickly decided that his imagination was running away with itself, no doubt because a moment before he had noticed two monks' habits lying seemingly discarded on the stone floor of the chapel, something that in itself was highly unusual.

One part of the abbey cathedral that was permanently blacked out was the twelfth century Lady Chapel and here the young fire-watcher was able to switch on an overhead light and pause before making the ascent up into the belfry of the massive Norman tower where he intended to watch the night sky for the possibility of a passing German air raid. As a precaution against possible damage from enemy bombing, the cathedral's twelve bells which at that time dated from between 1699 and 1935, had been removed from the belfry and were stored at the base of the tower. However, as Basil Saville approached the belfry door he was amazed to hear the deep tone of what could only be one of the cathedral bells begin to toll slowly, the sudden sound breaking the heavy silence that had previously hung inside the massive building. The one possibility that entered his mind, that one of the great bells had been re-erected inside the tower to act as an early warning of an impending air raid, was dashed when on opening the belfry door, the teenager saw that the great shafts that normally held the cathedral bells were empty and unmoving, at which point the mysterious and now unnerving sound faded away and the abbey became silent once more. Unsure just what he had experienced in the preceding minutes, the young fire-watcher crossed the empty loft and spent a short time outside on the tower roof before deciding to go back down to the ground floor and wait to see if any of the other regular platoon of fire-watchers had now arrived for the night watch. It is at this point that the teenager's experience becomes without doubt the most astonishing and perhaps for some readers, the most controversial case of haunting that we will encounter in the present survey.

Over forty years after the event, Basil Saville relived his experience for ghost hunter Betty Puttick. 'People may not believe me,' he stated, 'but I know it happened.' As he made his way back down through the tower into the main part of the cathedral, the teenager became aware of the sound of organ music which, like the mysterious bell ringing a short time before, began to fill the silence inside the vast and shadowy nave. Moving in the direction of the organ loft, Saville was alarmed to see what he took to be a light burning and, mindful of the strict rules concerning the wartime blackout, called out to whoever was practising at the organ to extinguish the light immediately. However, as he drew closer, he saw that the organist's seat at the console was empty and, like something out of a Gothic novel, both the organ keys were depressing by themselves and the pages of the music book that was open on the stand over the keyboard were slowly turning over, as though an invisible person was seated playing at the instrument. Before the impossibility of what he was witnessing had a chance to sink in, the young man's attention was suddenly drawn to the high altar of the cathedral and he found himself hurrying down the aisle of the nave as what Betty Puttick describes as a 'glorious burst of singing' came swirling out through the darkness. Saville claimed that as he approached the high altar the sounds of voices and music fell silent and he saw the solid figures of an abbot and a procession of hooded monks each holding a lighted candle, passing silently through the screen doors into the Saint's Chapel where he himself had had the uncanny feeling of being watched a short time before. The procession moved through the doorway and was lost to sight. When Saville made to follow them he found the screen doors closed. On opening them the chapel itself was still and in darkness. Of the silent monks there was no sign …

It was to be many years before Basil Saville revealed to the general public what allegedly happened to him that wartime Christmas Eve night. In 1982, he wrote to the local *Evening Post-Echo* newspaper in response to an appeal for seasonal stories and enclosed an account of his ghostly encounter. Saville was adamant that it was not a fictional tale; the experience happened exactly as he described, and thirty-eight years after the event he was still at a loss to explain it, just as he had been that very night. Saville confirmed other aspects of his story to Betty Puttick as published in the local newspaper: of finding a used candle beside the console in the organ lift which, like the two monks' cassocks which he had seen lying on the stone floor earlier in the evening, disappeared mysteriously when he and another fire-watcher (who turned up just after the cessation of the supernatural happenings) subsequently searched the building. Saville also claimed that the book of sheet music which he had found open on the organ and whose pages had turned mysteriously by themselves was a copy of the *Albanus Mass*, written by the sixteenth-century organist and former director of the abbey choir, Robert Fayrfax, who died in 1521 and is buried in the abbey crypt.

What actually took place in the vast and shadowy cathedral that night, we will never know for sure. Did the young fire-watcher have an encounter with the long-dead monks of the shrine of Alban the martyr? Was his experience some bizarre hallucination, or something totally beyond our understanding? Whatever the truth of the matter, the Abbey Church of St Alban was known locally as a haunted building well before Basil Saville's wartime experience, and all of the alleged phenomena said to have taken place there is connected with both ghostly music and the appearance of phantom monk-like figures. In 1933, during a lecture given to the St Albans Rotary Club, Mrs Francis Glossop of Romeland House claimed her late husband, Canon George Glossop, had heard ghostly music coming from the locked and closed abbey building while writing a sermon at their house several years before. The music seemed to swell to a great crescendo before gradually dying away. According to his wife, Canon Glossop claimed that he later recognised parts of the ghostly music as being compositions by Robert Fayrfax, whose *Albanus Mass* was the piece played by Basil Saville's invisible organist in 1944.

In 'St Albans Ghost Lore', Muriel Thresher and Beryl Carrington mention two more anecdotal accounts of supernatural happenings connected with the great abbey church. In the late 1930s, an abbey verger is said to have opened up the building early one morning in preparation for the first service of the day and was suddenly confronted by the arresting sight of a procession of Benedictine monks drifting silently towards him. The verger automatically moved to one side to allow the column to pass, but the figures became fainter and in the space of a few seconds had faded away into the surrounding stonework. In another undated incident, a lady living in one of the houses overlooking the abbey grounds – with a clear view of the great stained glass windows – is reported to have heard music coming from the building during the night hours when it was ostensibly locked and empty, and to have seen the glow of a single candle shining through one of the windows.

The shrine of the martyr St Alban. Fire-watcher Basil Saville claimed to have encountered a procession of phantom monks inside the Abbey Church during the closing months of the Second World War. (Eddie Brazil)

The Cross Keys public house in Harpenden, where a relief manager encountered the apparitions of three ghostly monks in the early 1960s. (Paul Adams)

Interestingly, another local haunting involving the appearance of monkish apparitions has been reported, not from a nearby abbey cell or similar monastic building, but a public house located in the town of Harpenden, which is 4.5 miles north of the city centre on the A1081. The Cross Keys, a late eighteenth-century hostelry constructed around an earlier timber-framed core, is reportedly built on land originally in the ownership of Westminster Abbey. In 1960, according to most published accounts, a relief manager on the premises was awoken one night, long after closing time, by the sound of voices and loud conversation coming from the ground floor of the building. Suspecting that the pub was being broken into, the unnamed manager made his way cautiously downstairs, but on looking in through the tap room door was stunned to see what appeared to be three monk-like figures in heavy dark-coloured robes grouped around one of the tables. At this point the group seemed to become aware of the manager's presence and as one they turned and looked towards him: all are described as having shaven crowns and the appearance of medieval monks. Terrified, the manager fled back up the stairs and subsequently refused to enter the tap room after dark. It has been suggested by Ruth Stratton and Nicholas Connell in *Haunted Hertfordshire* that the appearance of phantom monks at The Cross Keys had already happened prior to this incident, although no details are given, and that other odd occurrences of a paranormal nature took place there during the 1960s including the movement and disappearance of objects.

Given that the land on which The Cross Keys stands – despite an exceedingly protracted length of time – has links with an important religious establishment, it is not surprising that the apparitions allegedly seen there in 1960 were identified as being those of phantom monks, and it is true that the description given does seem to reinforce the identification. However, there is a possibility that this case, and many others of a similar nature reported across the country involving the sighting of ghostly monks and similar monkish apparitions, are not what they seem. Nor are the unquiet spirits or stone tape replays of long-dead religious ascetics manifesting in our continually technology-obsessed material world. Many sightings of monk-like apparitions take place in buildings and on land that have no associations or connections with religious houses or orders. In 1985 Sharon Grenny, a council tenant, was forced to flee with her family from their house in Sutcliffe Avenue, Grimsby, after several encounters with a sinister faceless apparition that she described as being a monk-like person with a wide hood drawn up obscuring its features. I researched two cases in 2011 involving a similar monkish figure in separate locations in Luton, Bedfordshire. In the late 1970s, Jennifer Davies reported experiencing poltergeist phenomena accompanied by appearances of a frightening monk-like figure with a disfigured face in a 1960s-built tower block in the Hockwell Ring estate, while on the other side of the town, a haunting of a semi-detached house (built by construction firm Laings in 1977) that again features a hooded figure in a brown habit-like costume, seen regularly in the vicinity of the staircase and first floor

landing, was ongoing when I included an account in *Haunted Luton and Dunstable*. In all three cases, there is no previous history of monastic buildings or activity in the area, which seems to suggest that these particular monk-like ghosts owe their appearances to whatever forces or stimuli create the paranormal hallucination and, perhaps more importantly, the way this hallucination is interpreted by the human mind.

Where sightings of apparitional figures are concerned, there is an interesting consistency across many reported hauntings that lends credence to paranormal incidents, which would otherwise be dismissed by the sceptics. I have noticed that many reports of ghostly figures that are seen at times in the most mundane of locations – ordinary houses and flats like the Luton hauntings mentioned above, as well as the more traditional stately homes and historic buildings – often appear 'faceless', or are described as having their faces covered or in some way obscured, although the components of the figure itself – arms, legs, torso etc. – are often seen and described in incredible and realistic detail. In neighbouring Bedfordshire, at Chicksands Priory near Shefford, researcher Damien O'Dell has described the appearance of a nun-like figure, seen by a psychic sensitive during a vigil inside the building. According to O'Dell, its facial features were blurred like a badly-tuned television set, although the figure's form and costume were clear and recognisable. An apparition seen in Battlefield House in Chequer Street in St Albans – which we will be looking at in more detail in the next chapter – is similarly described as being hatted but faceless in appearance. It would seem that whatever causes a ghost to appear, whether it be the mechanics of a spirit manifestation or an atmospheric photograph playback, can at times have difficulties in recreating the face and facial features, the most expressive and individual part of the human form, and on these occasions only achieve a more generalised or generic recreation. A glance through a number of the reported hauntings in the present survey do involve apparitional figures with recognisable faces: in the case of the haunting of The Goat public house, only the ghost's face itself was seen, although the haunting manifested itself in other ways, including noises and the movement of objects. Clearly the 'rules', as it were, of paranormal phenomena and the appearance of ghostly forms and figures are many and varied, and at the present time – and perhaps for all time – will be beyond our knowledge. Some of the St Albans ghosts included in this book may well follow the general pattern described above, but as many sightings are now historic and their witnesses unknown, further investigation and re-evaluation is now impossible.

Although many of our churches and ecclesiastical buildings have long-established paranormal histories, the attitude of many members of the church authorities to the idea of ghostly phenomena in these places is in the main one of indifference, and at times, resentment and opposition. The reasons are both practical and theological. Where parishes possess ruined church buildings that inevitably become the target of thrill-seekers and vandalism, it is understandable that stories of alleged hauntings and requests by reputable paranormal groups to carry out investigations are both rejected and refused. A local example of this is the old church of St Mary's at Clophill, just off the A6 trunk road between Luton and Bedford, where graveyard desecrations in the early 1960s have drawn occultists and sensationalists in equal numbers over many years. Further north in Northamptonshire, the ruins of St John the Baptist church at Boughton are said to be haunted at Christmas time by at least two ghosts: an apparition of a woman with red hair, and the moaning ghost of George Catherall, a local highwayman known as 'Captain Slash' who was hanged at Northampton in 1826 for robbery. Both sites have had their fair share of problems created by unwanted visitors and there are several other cases, such as the church at Borley in Essex, long associated with the famous 'most haunted house in England', where tales of ghosts and haunting rankle with the church authorities.

Another form of opposition comes from the orthodox teachings of the Christian church itself, which rejects the idea of unquiet spirits in preference to a belief that the souls of the departed find peace and eventual resurrection in the presence of God. This creed suffered perhaps its greatest challenge with the establishment of Modern Spiritualism which began in New York State in America in 1848 and quickly spread to Europe and around the world. Spritualism, mediumship and the associated practices of the séance room were firmly condemned by the Church of England for many years. However, in 1938, an enquiry was instigated by the then Archbishop of Canterbury, Dr Cosmo Lang, who was persuaded by

Dr Cosmo Lang (1864–1945), former Archbishop of Canterbury, who instigated an examination of spiritualism and mediumship in the 1930s.

the Archbishop of York, William Temple, to establish a ten-strong committee to examine claims for spirit communication, mental and physical mediumship and survival after death. The panel of investigators, which included several learned theologians and clerics, spent twelve months producing what eventually turned out to be two separate documents: a majority report favourable to Spiritualism, and a shorter minority report by three members of the panel who 'wished to reserve their opinions against the possibility that future discoveries might provide alternative explanations to Spiritualistic hypotheses'. These reports were suppressed for several years until both were leaked to the Spiritualist newspaper *Psychic News* in 1947. An account of both the formation of the Church of England report and its eventual publication is given by former *Psychic News* editor and journalist Fred Archer in his book *Exploring the Psychic World*. Despite this orthodox resistance, and in the aftermath of the revelations of the Church of England report on Spiritualism in the late 1940s, the Churches' Fellowship for Psychic Study, now the Churches' Fellowship for Psychical and Spiritual Studies, was established in 1953 to promote the study of psychical and religious experiences within a basic Christian context. The Fellowship organises lectures and study groups and produces two regular publications, the *Christian Parapsychologist* and the *Quarterly Review*.

One building associated with the abbey church which is almost crying out for a ghost but for which surprisingly no paranormal records exist, is the ruined Sopwell Priory, founded around the middle of the twelfth century as the Priory of St Mary of Sopwell, a cell of the nearby abbey. Also known as Sopwell Nunnery, the fifteenth-century writer Juliana Berners, authoress of *The Boke of Saint Albans*, a compilation of hunting, hawking and heraldry, is thought at one time to have been a prioress here. In 1539, Sir Richard Lee, a military surveyor and engineer, seized the opportunity afforded by the Dissolution of the Monasteries, and purchased the priory and its grounds for his own use. He quickly demolished the existing buildings and built a Tudor manor house which he named Lee Hall after himself. This was later renamed Sopwell House, and following Sir Richard's death in 1575, the estate passed to other members of the Lee family, who held it for over a century before finally selling the property in the mid-1600s to the

Sopwell Priory, St Albans: ghostly ruins that appear to lack a ghost. (Eddie Brazil)

politician Sir Harbottle Grimston, who in 1660 held the position of Speaker of the House of Commons. Sir Harbottle's main residence was Gorhambury, a large house built 100 years before by Sir Nicholas Bacon, Lord Keeper of the Great Seal, on the outskirts of Prae Wood. Sopwell House was used for building materials to refurbish this more favoured dwelling. The Lee family house was subsequently reduced to a shell, in a similar way that Houghton House in neighbouring Bedfordshire, itself an allegedly haunted building (see William King's book *Haunted Bedfordshire: A Ghostly Compendium* for the full case history), was plundered at the end of the eighteenth century.

It remains a picturesque ruin to this day. The full history of Sopwell Priory is given by Donald Pelletier in his book *Mysterious Ruins: The Story of Sopwell Priory, St Albans*. The only vaguely ghostly tale associated with Sopwell has been collected by Ruth Stretton and Nicholas Connell in *Haunted Hertfordshire: A Ghostly Gazetteer*, and involves the death of the bridegroom of a young woman named Lilian, a ward of Sopwell Nunnery, who was murdered by her brothers on his way to be married at St Albans Abbey in 1872. The unfortunate man's ghost is said to have appeared at the wedding party at which the poor Lilian, already robbed of her beloved, died of shock. The tale is a pretty one but its setting in Victorian times, by which time the Priory of St Mary had been long gone, makes it no more than an interesting anecdote for a site that lacks a verifiable haunting of its own. It is worth mentioning that an unsolved murder took place nearby in 1948 when the body of Stephen Varley, a shop steward from Hatfield, was found dead on an allotment close to the Nunnery Stables.

As for the ghosts of the Abbey Church of St Albans, whether new reports of phenomena occurring here will come to light remains to be seen. The abbey is just one of the city's many ancient and historical buildings that have a connection with the twilight world of the unseen, and in the next part of our survey we will spend some time examining a number of these interesting and convincing cases.

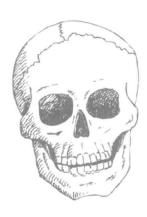

4

HAUNTED HOUSES AND BUILDINGS

OR our first stop on a tour of some of St Albans' notable haunted houses we do not have to stray far from the precincts of the great Abbey Church. In fact, the impressive flint rubble and brick structure known as the Abbey Gateway, which spans Abbey Mill Lane to the west of the cathedral is, apart from the church itself, all that now remains of the former Benedictine monastery. In the early 1870s, the building was taken over by the prestigious St Albans School, not only the oldest school in Hertfordshire but one of the oldest in the country, which can trace its origins back to the tenth century. The gateway itself was constructed around 1365 and comprises a number of rooms spread over three storeys; a pitched and tiled roof was added in the seventeenth century, and shortly afterwards it became a school building. The west elevation was extended in 1892. Following the Dissolution of the Monasteries, the Abbey Gateway had been used as a prison, and it is from this period of its history lasting for 300 years

that its haunted reputation appears to originate. Disembodied screams, seemingly psychic imprints of former inmates, together with the opening and closing of windows and possibly doors are said to have been encountered in the past, but like many reports from allegedly haunted buildings, named witnesses and dated experiences are lacking, something that anyone with more than a passing interest in researching the paranormal will be quite familiar with.

Within sight of the haunted Abbey Gateway on Romeland Hill is a line of late eighteenth-century cottages, where the appearance of a monk-like figure in the early part of the 1900s has been reported. In 1903, the Skeat family moved into one of the houses shortly before the birth of their son, Francis, who went on to become a noted English glass painter. One evening, the Skeats' Swedish maid, Hilma, was retiring to bed when she was overcome by an invisible force that pinned her against the wall of the stairwell and at the same time extinguished the candle she was holding.

The Abbey Gateway, a former prison, said to be haunted by the sounds of screaming men. (Eddie Brazil)

In the dim half-light, the frightened girl became aware of a cowled figure that seemed to step out from the nearby wall and began to speak in a tongue that she was unable to understand. The vision lasted for only a few seconds before it and the mysterious pressure holding her against the side of the stairway vanished. The following night, Hilma awoke in the early hours of the morning and again saw the same monkish apparition standing at the foot of her bed. Whether the figure spoke a second time is unclear, but there was apparently enough moon-light filtering in through the bedroom window for her to make out the shape of a distinctive metal medallion hanging around the apparition's neck. As before, the figure quickly faded away and the young Hilma found herself alone in the room. If the apparition appeared to the young woman again, then the incident has gone unrecorded. Most accounts of this haunting close with the mysterious language being identified as Latin and the design of the metal medal correspond-ing with that of pilgrimage medallions given to visitors to the abbey during the Middle Ages. Francis Skeat went on to complete several dozen church window

Romeland Cottage, adjacent to the grounds of the Abbey Church, where the apparition of a monkish figure was seen during the occupation of the Skeat family in the early 1900s. (Eddie Brazil)

commissions across the country, including depictions of St John the Baptist and The Good Shepherd in St Albans abbey, the arms of Baron Beaverbrook in St Michael's church in Mickleham in Surrey, a memorial window to the Revd Robinson Duckworth (who was one of the first people to hear the adventures of Alice as told in person by Lewis Carroll) in Westminster Abbey, and the Rose Window in St George's Cathedral, Cape Town, South Africa.

In an earlier part of this book we looked at reports of ghostly sounds and noises, allegedly psychic playbacks of the First Battle of St Albans, which are said to have been heard in the vicinity of Holywell Hill on occasions in the past. This is a haunting that has direct connections with what was probably at one time

the city's most famous haunted building, the appropriately titled Battlefield House that was located further to the north, where Holywell Hill runs into Chequer Street. An Elizabethan half-timbered building, Battlefield House is traditionally thought to have stood near to the defence line of the Duke of Somerset and his Lancastrian forces, with the result that for many years the sounds of galloping horses, the ring of swords on armour and other noises of combat were heard by various occupants and visitors. The chanting of monks was another auditory phenomenon said to have been encountered here, as was the somewhat sinister apparition of a face-less man wearing a caped greatcoat and beaver hat, described as a 'family ghost' by a local resident who lived for a time

Chequer Street looking south towards Holywell Hill in the early 1900s. The twin-gabled façade of much haunted Battlefield House can be seen on the left.

in Battlefield House as a child. As well as a private residence, the haunted building saw use as a school as well as a shop on the ground floor before being demolished in the 1970s when the site was redeveloped and infilled with a new building. Despite its status as a well-known haunted house, stories of ghostly activity here are very much anecdotal in nature, and with the original building gone, a modern reassessment is now no longer possible.

In May 1901, a local tailor named Mr W.S. Green who owned other properties in Chequer Street took a lease on Battlefield House in order to expand his existing business. He carried out some substantial alterations in order to bring the place up to modern standards. The original red-brick façade was taken down and replaced with a twin-gabled front elevation constructed in a

similar half-timbered style, with a new shopfront in black and gold with pillars and stallriser faced in Aberdeen granite. Through a report of the building work in a clipping from an unnamed newspaper held at the St Albans Museum, it is possible to locate the site of the former Battlefield House, which despite being a well-known haunted landmark, does not appear in either any of the city's published histories, the Council-produced survey of Chequer Street, or the museum's own collection of information on Tudor St Albans. In 1902, Mr Green's store was listed as occupying Nos 2, 3, 5, 7 and 9 Chequer Street, just up from the crossroads junction with the High Street and London Road. In 1996, the building was converted into The Cross Keys public house by the J.D. Wetherspoon pub chain, who remained on the site until March 2012.

Moving away from Chequer Street towards the southern side of the city is the site of another of the lost haunted buildings of St Albans, which today, like Battlefield House, no longer exists. In the mid-1960s, the Mandeville children's home was built on the St Julians estate, over an area of playing field off Holyrood Crescent, adjacent to what is now Watling View School. The home was closed in the early 2000s and a development of modern houses called Remus Close now occupies the site. It was here in 1974 that Biggleswade resident Jo Clarke, then aged 8, had an unnerving encounter with the supernatural. One evening as she made her way up the main staircase inside the building, Jo turned a bend on the stairs, and on one of the half-landings came face to face with what can only be described as a semi-human figure. The apparition was black and shaped 'like a tree' but with half a human face that was turned towards her. Unable to comprehend what she was seeing, the child screamed and ran back down the stairs. When members of the children's home staff checked the staircase a few minutes later, there was no sign of the sinister half-formed figure in black. The child's vision brings to mind the concept of the Green Man, an ancient nature symbol often depicted as a part-man, part-tree figure with a human face wreathed in leaves or surmounted with branches, but rather than being a benign representation of the natural world around us, this apparition gave off a distinct aura of sinister menace. Before Jo Clarke's experience, nothing out of the ordinary had been seen or heard before on the main staircase, but another part of the building was regarded by several of the Mandeville children as being haunted. This was a ground floor laundry area linking the children's home with a hostel for older girls located on the same site. Several of the hostel girls were unwilling to spend time in the laundry room, particularly after dark, although whether anything was actually seen or experienced there is unclear.

Writing in *The Ghost Hunter's Guide* that we have briefly discussed at the start of our survey, Peter Underwood has commented that statistically it has been suggested that we all have a one-in-ten chance of seeing a ghost at some time during the course of our lives. However, when one examines many reports of paranormal experiences, it seems that for a certain proportion of the population, these odds are significantly increased: a number of people have many supernatural encounters during their lifetimes, often beginning in childhood. Jo Clarke is one such person who, it would seem – like many psychically endowed people – sees ghosts when she is least expecting them, and often in the most ordinary and mundane of situations, as the following example shows. One evening, many years after her experience in St Albans, Jo was delivering pizzas to an address in the small village of Broom, 1.5 miles south-west of the centre of Biggleswade. Ringing the doorbell of the house on the delivery ticket, she was surprised when a small boy with blond hair wearing a blue jumper opened the door and looked out at her, before quickly stepping back inside and closing the door. Thinking that the child was playing a game, Jo rang the doorbell again. After a minute or so a young woman came to the door and paid for the pizza. When Jo mentioned that her son had beaten her to the door, the customer was somewhat surprised: she had no children, there was no small blond boy in the flat and she herself had only moved there just over two weeks before …

From strange and modern ghosts, we move further into the centre of St Albans to examine several haunted buildings in one of the city's most well-known thoroughfares. St Peter's Street, described in the mid-1240s as the 'great street', and running from the triangular-shaped and at one time much larger Market Place in the south to the twelfth-century church which gives it its name at the northern end, is an ancient road. In the fourteenth century, parts of the borough boundary were delineated by a defensive earthwork comprising two ditches and mounds, and dwellings lining the route of St Peter's Street stretched back to these protective lines: Tonman Ditch, or Monk Ditch, to the east, and Houndspath to the west. Over the centuries the road has seen much development and redevelopment: medieval buildings have been replaced with those from later times, and several of the Georgian period houses which at one time were prevalent have now gone. The northern section of St Peter's Street was at one time known as Bowgate, a corruption – possibly – of 'borough gate', and in the fourteenth century was likely to have been pasture land; later, at the end of the century, several crofts occupied the area. Here, opposite St Peter's Church, is an early eighteenth-century building with a famous connection to English architecture and church history. No. 107 St Peter's Street, a building formerly known as Electricity House but which today goes under the name of Ivy House, was built by Edward Strong, who along with his elder brother Thomas was a chief mason to Sir Christopher Wren on the construction of St Paul's Cathedral. The Strong brothers laid the first stone at the new St Paul's in June 1675, and it came into use twenty-two years later when Henry Compton, the then Bishop of London, preached the first sermon on 2 December 1697. Strong's residence in St Albans, now a listed structure like many buildings across the city, is an impressive three-storey house with a columned entrance. Ivy House has since been extended on either side and occupies the site of an earlier building. It is from here that the origins of its haunted reputation lie.

Since the early 2000s, the legal firm of Debenhams Ottaway has occupied Ivy House, and following an enquiry, their Chief Executive Ian Hopkins told me that they have experienced nothing out of the ordinary during the time they have been there. However, previous writers on St Albans' ghosts including Muriel Thresher, Beryl Carrington and Damien O'Dell, suggest that in previous years things were not so quiet. Former occupants were both troubled and assisted here by the ghost of a murdered servant girl by the name of Meades. She was allegedly immured alive within a wall of the previous building to stand on the site as a brutal punishment for becoming pregnant by an unnamed member of the household, who chose to bury his indiscretion rather than pay maintenance. It is the spirit of the tragic chambermaid that in previous years has seemingly haunted the rooms and corridors of Ivy House, particularly the main staircase, where her presence has most often been felt. Here the banister rail is said to have been kept mysteriously

Ivy House, where the unhappy ghost of a former servant girl haunts the staircase. (Eddie Brazil)

clean, even during refurbishment work when the entire building became coated in dust, the inference being that the tragic young domestic was giving the cleaners on this side of life a helping hand from beyond the grave. As preposterous as this may sound, the presence of a female apparition inside the building, seen on at least two occasions by separate members of staff, seems to give this particular haunting more credence than the story of the cleaning ghost would at first appear to warrant. In 1975, a manager returning one evening to collect some papers from his office saw the figure of a young, blond-haired woman in a white dress standing on one of the upper floor landings. The apparition glanced in the manager's direction before walking out of sight up the next flight of stairs, at which point the office worker, unnerved by his experience, turned and left. On another occasion, the same sad-looking figure was seen by several members of staff who had come into the office out of hours to decorate a Christmas tree. Again, the apparition was seen in the stairwell area of the building, where several cleaners are also said to have heard footsteps and other unusual noises while working on the premises. Damien O'Dell also reports poltergeist-type phenomena taking place, including the opening and closing of doors as well as basin and sink taps being turned on and off. It is perhaps worth mentioning that there is a suggestion that the haunted staircase in Ivy House may possibly have been carved by the famous sculptor and English

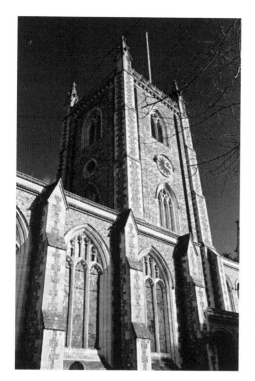

St Peter's Church, allegedly the haunt of the first ghost of St Albans. (Eddie Brazil)

craftsman Grinling Gibbons, whose work includes the palaces of Blenheim and Hampton Court as well as St Paul's Cathedral and the church of St Michael Paternoster Royal.

The church of St Peter noted above is worth more than a passing mention, as it was here that what appears to be the earliest sighting of an apparition in the town took place in the middle of the thirteenth century. In 1258, the figure of an old man with a long flowing beard is said to have appeared to an anchorite at the top of the church tower, and prophesised the onset of a great famine that would spread across the country. This supernatural prophecy eventually came true, as widespread pestilence and famine are known to have afflicted many parts of the northern hemisphere

around this time; disasters that were at one time considered as being due to immense volcanic activity now thought to have occurred thousands of miles away in Indonesia.

It was in 2002 while enquiring into a potential mortgage application that I first became acquainted with another of St Peter's Street's haunted buildings, The Grange, located on the opposite side from Ivy House and a short walk back towards the city centre, close to the new council offices and the Alban Arena entertainment venue. Occupied by the Nationwide Building Society for several years, The Grange was constructed in 1763 by John Osborne, a local dignitary and alderman who held the position of Mayor of St Albans on three separate occasions. He died on 1 October 1799, shortly after his third and final stint in office had come to a close and is buried in nearby Harpenden. Many years after his death, Mayor Osborne's house acquired a haunted reputation, possibly beginning in the 1940s, when – following the Second World War – it came into the ownership of St Albans Council. Office typists and the resident caretaker became unnerved on several occasions, although there appear to be no records of their actual experiences. However, in 1975 the then caretaker is quoted as encountering an 'eerie, icy atmosphere' while alone in the basement area, during which he became aware of an unseen presence that disappeared after he turned on all the lights. A corridor on the first floor of the building is particularly noted as one of the most haunted areas. It was here that Nationwide staff told me of the figure of a woman in a long grey dress being seen on occasion. Like many sightings of apparitions, the appearance of

One of several haunted buildings in St Peter's Street, The Grange is haunted by the apparition of a silent woman in grey. (Eddie Brazil)

Mallinson House in St Peter's Street, formerly known as Donnington House. In 1872, the sighting of a mysterious apparition in an upstairs window drew a crowd of over 200 people. (Paul Adams)

the Grey Lady is brief and often visible for just a few seconds, in this case seen in the act of turning the corner at the end of the corridor where, during the time I visited, a photocopier was located. This particular ghost has become known as Dorothy Osborne, said to be a daughter-in-law of Mayor Osborne; she committed suicide after it was revealed that her husband was having an affair. Research into the genealogy of the Osborne family has challenged this particular notion but whatever her origins, The Grange's Grey Lady is still seen by staff from time to time.

Close by The Grange and occupying nos 38–42 St Peter's Street is Mallinson House, today the registered offices of the National Pharmacy Association. Another late eighteenth century building, this was originally known as Donnington House, and for several years was the residence of a local surgeon, Dr William Russell. After his death, his former home was briefly in the headlines when the sighting of an apparition at one of the windows one evening in 1872 drew a large crowd of sightseers which eventually had to be broken up by police. An article entitled 'Ghost at St Albans' which appeared shortly afterwards in the *Herts Advertiser* concerning the incident is worth quoting in full. This is based on the transcription included by Thresher and Carrington in *St Albans Ghost Lore*:

A ghost is a luxury we are seldom nowadays permitted to indulge in; St Albans, however, is fortunate in this respect, for on Sunday evening about 7 p.m. – not by any means a ghostly hour – some imaginative person while passing the [Donnington] house occupied by the late Dr. Russell, saw, or fancied he saw, a figure wearing a white hat at one of the upper windows. He at once called the attention of passers by [sic], who appeared to be as equally credulous as himself and soon a crowd of about 200 would-be ghost-seers collected around the house, where they waited with the most exemplary patience for some two or three hours. Few, however, were favoured with another view of the ghostly occupant, although one old lady was most positive in her assertion that she had seen 'something'; others only heard taps at the window, while another of the crowd, more fortunate than the rest, actually heard the ghost speak, although what it said has not yet transpired.

It is to be regretted that this pleasing illusion should have been dispelled by some sceptical members of the Police force who entered and examined the house. However, notwithstanding the most careful search of every part they could not discover the slightest trace of the intruder, and subsequent investigation led to the conclusion that the house was entered from the back by someone intent on having a 'lark'.

It would seem that the building, closed and apparently empty following the death of Dr Russell, had garnered a local reputation as a haunted house. The sighting of a figure at the window was considered at the time to be both unusual and supernatural in nature. Was this the ghost of William Russell's unnamed former butler, who is said to have committed suicide in an upper room of the house through guilt at being caught drinking his master's brandy, or, as the St Albans police suspected at

Site of the much haunted Wellington public house, now redeveloped. Accounts of ghostly activity including footsteps and the appearance of phantom figures stretch back over several decades. (Eddie Brazil)

the time, a local youngster 'ghosting for a giggle'? We will never know for sure. Just over 100 years later, Mallinson House was the scene of another alleg-edly ghostly experience, when in 1977 a builder on the premises claimed to have seen the apparition of a legless man, who passed him briefly on the main staircase. This is in direct contrast to an account in the 'most haunted' city of York, where the Black Swan Inn is said to be haunted by a pair of disembodied male legs which have been seen on occasion descending a staircase inside the pub. Reports of a light phenomenon seen at regular intervals at one of the first floor windows of Mallinson House have also been collected by Damien O'Dell in his *Paranormal Hertfordshire*.

Returning along St Peter's Street to the Market Place gives us the opportu-nity to examine the history and ghosts of

one of St Albans' most unusual haunted buildings, one that at first is not readily apparent. This is the site of the former Wellington public house, now rede-veloped and rebuilt as a retail outlet currently occupied by the Specsavers opticians chain. Prior to 1972, the build-ing had a long history as a hostelry going back several hundred years, and in the eighteenth century was known as the Blue Boar. It was during this time that a local boy known as Charlie is said to have been struck down and killed by a coach turning into the stable yard, and it is his unquiet spirit that was allegedly seen and felt by many people over the years, up until the late 1960s. Phenomena experienced by both staff and customers included the movement of objects, the sound of heavy furni-ture being moved about in parts of the building known to be empty at the time, disembodied footsteps, psychic touches and other tactile experiences – a barmaid claimed to have been kissed on the fore-head by an invisible person and felt small hands stroking her hair – while room lights would on occasion turn on and off by themselves.

By the beginning of the 1970s, the intensity of the haunting of the Wellington had reduced somewhat. Mr and Mrs Tew, who held the licence at the time, experienced odd happen-ings – footfalls on the stairs and in an upstairs corridor – but things in a para-normal sense were particularly quiet, and during their time on the prem-ises, neither the Tews nor their staff saw either an apparition or any other kind of visual phenomenon. In October 1971, shortly before the Wellington closed its doors for good, new landlords Mr and Mrs Jupp moved into No. 26 Market

Place. During the time that they were there, and seemingly invigorated by a change in licensee, the unseen ghosts of the Wellington became active again, and the building became infested with – at times – alarming poltergeist-type activity: objects in the tap room were moved, and on one occasion the gas supply to the beer engines had seemingly turned off by itself. Bottles, glasses and ale jugs were found smashed on the floor, and one member of the Jupps' staff claimed that doors opened in front of her as if she was preceded by an invisible person as she moved through the pub. Mr and Mrs Jupp also experienced the sound of footsteps on the main staircase and along one of the upstairs passages, in the same way that the Tews were aware of the movement of their unseen occupant.

In September 1972, the Jupps left the Wellington and from that time the premises ceased to trade as a public house. Major building work involved in the creation of the Christopher Place shopping centre saw the original pub building demolished and a new three-storey development was erected on the site, although the parts of the original Wellington cellars were retained and incorporated into the new design. For several years the new No. 26 Market place address was owned by the Matthews butchers' chain, and despite the drastic change of environment, ghostly phenomena continued to be reported on the site. In the old cellar, a young apprentice butcher claimed to see the hazy apparition of a male figure, the first time that such a phenomenon had occurred in the history of the case, although due to the poor light he was unable to make out any particular details at the time. Later,

another apparition was seen: a male figure, standing with its arms folded in the yard area at the rear of the shop at around half past five in the morning. Both members of the Matthews staff and customers in the shop complained of psychic touches, akin to the feeling of cobwebs brushing their faces; items inside the ground floor shop were also moved and interfered with. One aspect of this particular period of the haunting, namely the vandalism of the car tyres of vehicles parked at the back of shop, which at the time were put down to the ghost, are somewhat hard to believe and it seems more likely to be due to normal causes, perhaps someone playing up the ghostly history of the premises for their own amusement. That is not to say that some cases of haunting, most specifically those involving poltergeist-type manifestations, do not feature instances of destructive behaviour and vandalism on the part of the 'ghost'. Notable examples are at Pontefract – the notorious Black Monk case – in the late 1960s and at Enfield in north London in 1977 (see my book *Extreme Hauntings* for detailed examinations of both these cases). The haunting of No. 26 Market Place is one that continues to manifest into modern times. In *Haunted Hertfordshire*, Ruth Stratton and Nicholas Connell report continued activity on the site of the old haunted public house: room lights and heating equipment switching on and off, as well as psychic touches and the movement of objects, were reported to the authors during the time that they were compiling their book.

The continued manifestation of psychic phenomena on the site of the former Wellington public house, despite the demolition of the original building and the erection of new shop premises, challenges certain aspects of the stone tape theory. In the case of No. 26 Market Place, one might possibly expect that the ghostly happenings would have come to a close once the original building had been removed. The fact that phenomena have continued to be reported in a similar vein here for a number of years since the redevelopment of the site makes it likely that some hauntings are possibly due to the interaction of the human mind with naturally-occurring forces (like the natural 'energy' fields that create the ley line phenomenon), present either in the earth itself or at that particular location, and as such will continue to manifest regardless of the building or structure physically present. This may well explain why some modern buildings built on green field

Mountfitchet Castle, Essex. This ghostly image of a hooded figure was captured by paranormal investigators on the night of 18 July 2010. The author and his family experienced unusual sensations of giddiness and touching on the same spot in the summer of 2012. (Mountfitchet Castle)

sites or areas not known to have been previously developed become haunted, or why the people living or working in them experience apparitions and other forms of psychic phenomena. An interesting example involving myself and members of my family in the summer of 2012 is worth briefly relating here.

During the school summer holiday, I took three of my children to Mountfitchet Castle, an open-air museum on the site of a Norman motte and bailey castle, 2 miles north-west of Stanstead Airport in Essex. The original buildings have long since perished, although some small sections of a previous Saxon fortification, around which the later Norman castle was constructed in 1066, still remain. Several modern reconstructions of parts of the Norman castle have been erected around the museum including the Grand Hall that contains recreations of the local baron's banqueting table, armoury and sleeping quarters. I am not normally sensitive to psychic happenings, which goes some way to explaining my sceptical outlook on many allegedly paranormal happenings, and on a previous visit to Mountfitchet I had not experienced anything out of the ordinary. However, on this occasion, while pausing to read an information notice next to a doorway leading from the ground floor banqueting hall through into the adjacent armoury room, I quickly became aware of an uncomfortable feeling in this particular part of the building, akin to a close and unpleasant pressure about my head and a sensation of giddiness which made me feel as though I was standing on the tilting deck of a ship at sea. All three of my children felt uncomfortable in the same area at the same time:

my thirteen-year-old son Idris complained of similar feelings to my own, my youngest son Isa felt a sudden feeling of nausea and his sister Sakina described a sensation as though someone were pushing her forcibly in the small of the back. When we passed through the doorway into the adjacent room, these spontaneous sensations quickly vanished and several other visitors present in the Grand Hall at the same time were unaffected when passing through this same spot. Interestingly, two years before, during the night of 18 July 2010 when the building was closed and empty, a remotely-operated infrared camera captured what appeared to be the image of a hooded monk-like figure, standing close to where my family and I had our unusual experience. In this particular case, the 'stone tape' theory of haunting is unsatisfactory as the buildings present are of comparatively recent origin and it seems likely that here, as at the site of the old Wellington public house in St Albans, naturally occurring forces present on the site may be interacting in some unknowable way with the human mind, creating unnatural sensations and the appearance of phantom figures.

Returning to St Albans, we can again open the case files of ghost hunter Tony Broughall to look briefly at an historic haunting in Grosvenor Road, a street that has seen much alteration and redevelopment over the years. During the first half of the twentieth century, the Edwin Lee & Sons Ltd boot and shoe factory operated from premises in Grosvenor Road before closing in the early 1950s. Later, an office building (now demolished) occupied the same site and was used for several years by the Schweppes drinks company as a regional office. It was here in the late summer of 1978 that cleaning staff began to complain of strange happenings centred around a suite of offices on the seventh floor of the building. Reports of localised sensations of coldness and feelings of a 'presence', as well as the opening and slamming of doors, were reported over a number of weeks. On one occasion, a cleaner and a work shift supervisor were present when a door slammed shut close behind them; an immediate inspection revealed the entire floor to be completely empty. At the time it was suggested that the disturbances were due to the unquiet spirit of a former employee of the Lee factory who committed suicide on the site, but like many cases, the background to the explanation is difficult to prove, and the haunting itself ended as suddenly as it began. The site itself has now been redeveloped.

For our final haunted building we move just over three and a half miles south-east of St Albans city centre to the rolling countryside close to the stretch of the M25 motorway near London Colney, a site steeped in English history as well as ghostly associations – the seventeenth-century manor house of Salisbury Hall, well known today for its connection with the de Havilland aircraft company. In the years before the Norman Conquest, the land formed part of the Manor of Shenleybury, held by the Saxon courtier Asgar the Staller. Later, after William the Conqueror's victory at Hastings, ownership passed to the 1st Earl of Essex, the robber knight Geoffrey de Mandeville, who was arrested in St Albans in 1143 for treason against King Stephen. Eventually killed by an arrow during the siege of Burwell Castle in Cambridgeshire the following

Salisbury Hall, on the outskirts of London Colney, now a private residence. Accounts of supernatural activity, including encounters with phantom figures, stretch back to the early 1900s. (Peter Underwood Collection)

year, de Mandeville's ghost, dressed in full battle armour including a red-plumed helmet and matching cloak, is said to haunt the roads between East Barnet village and South Mimms, materialising at Christmas time every six years with a spectral dog at his heels. Ghost hunter Tony Broughall has calculated that his next appearance will be in 2018.

In 1380, Sir John Montague, later to become the Earl of Salisbury, married into the de Mandeville family, and his elevation to the peerage ultimately gave the estate the name it has been known by for many centuries. In the early fifteenth century, Lady Alice Montecute, Countess of Salisbury, married Sir Richard Neville, later the Earl of Warwick. She bore him two sons: John, Marquis of Montague, and Richard, the 16th Earl and better known today as Warwick the Kingmaker. Both men fell at the Battle of Barnet on 14 April 1471 and their bodies were subsequently put on display in St Paul's Cathedral before being laid to rest at Bisham Priory in Berkshire. Following their deaths, Salisbury Hall fell into decline to the point that when Sir John Cutte, treasurer to both Henry VII and Henry VIII, bought the property around 1507, he demolished the extant buildings and replaced them with a fine new moated house. This building survived until the latter years of the seventeenth century, during which time several members of the Cutte family made it their home.

In 1668, Richard Cole, who had bought the house in 1617, sold it for

£7,100 to a London banker, James Hoare. The following year, another financier, Sir Jeremy Snow, together with his wife Rebecca, took up ownership. Snow, like Richard Cole, was a close friend of Charles II, and he undertook an ambitious programme of alteration work, tearing down the main house and replacing it with the building which stands on the site today. The Snows effectively acted as housekeepers during visits to the estate by the King and his long-time mistress, the actress Eleanor 'Nell' Gwynne. In the grounds of the hall overlooking the moat, Snow built a small oak-beamed house which today is still known as Nell Gwynne's Cottage. It was here that Eleanor reputedly dangled her first child by the King, Charles Beauclerk, by the leg over the moat from a window and threatened to drop him into the water unless he was granted a suitable title. Seeing the outline of St Albans Abbey in the distance, the King is said to have relented with the words, 'No, spare the 1st Duke of St Albans!' There are several variations of this story and Charles was in actuality granted the title at the age of fourteen. Charles II continued his illicit liaisons at Salisbury Hall for several years until his death in 1684; Nell followed her lover to the grave three years later, dying at her London house in Pall Mall on the evening of 14 November 1687 at the age of 37. Jeremy Snow's nephew, John, later took up ownership and for many years the story of Salisbury Hall becomes rather more mundane: the estate passed through the hands of several farming families until the opening decade of the twentieth century when, in 1905, it was bought by the widowed Lady Randolph Churchill and her new husband, the Scots Guardsman, George Cornwallis-West.

The ownership of the Cornwallis-Wests ushered in an era of Edwardian opulence at Salisbury Hall: Winston Churchill often stayed with his mother and stepfather and King Edward VII was a regular guest, as were several well-known personalities of the day, including the Italian actress Eleonora Duse and singer Dame Nellie Melba. During the 1930s up until the outbreak of war, the steam locomotive engineer Sir Nigel Gresley of the London and North Eastern Railway, designer of the famous *Flying Scotsman* and other record-breaking trains including *Mallard*, the fastest stream train in the world, owned the estate. However, in September 1939, Gresley's team vacated the Hall and made way for the de Havilland Aircraft Company whose prototype Mosquito fighter-bomber was designed and constructed in outbuildings adjacent to the main house.

Nell Gwynne (1650–87), mistress to Charles II. An apparition, said to be her ghost, has been seen at Salisbury Hall by several people over the years.

The Mosquito went into mass production in the summer of 1941 and the de Havilland organisation stayed on at Salisbury Hall until 1947 after which the estate again fell into disrepair. Eventually, in the mid-1950s, after several years of neglect, it was bought by Walter Goldsmith, an ex-Royal Marine turned art dealer, who together with his wife set out on an ambitious period of restoration. The Goldsmiths also opened the house to the public and re-established Salisbury Hall's wartime aircraft heritage. The Goldsmiths left in 1981 and today the de Havilland Aircraft Heritage Centre, first established by Water Goldsmith in 1959, operates from a series of hangers built in the grounds of the estate.

For many years, from the time of the Cornwallis-Wests onwards, reports of ghosts and phantom figures have become part of the history of this remarkable property. The appearance of one female apparition has, not surprisingly given her association with the estate, been identified as being that of the illustrious Royal mistress, Nell Gwynne, one of the earliest surviving reports being credited to Winston Churchill's stepfather during the years before the First World War. One afternoon, while passing through the oak-panelled entrance hall, a part of the building known as the Great Chamber, George Cornwallis-West became aware of the figure of what he later described as an attractive young woman wearing a blue fichu about her shoulders. The woman appeared to be watching him intently, but when the former soldier went to walk towards her, she turned and moved away into a corridor leading to another part of the house. Cornwallis-West followed but

quickly realised that the woman had disappeared and was nowhere to be seen, despite a search. At the time, Cornwallis-West assumed that he had experienced a 'crisis' ghost and that the apparition was that of Ellen Bryan, a former nursemaid to the family, who he felt must have died. However, after contacting his mother, it was established that Ellen was very much alive and at the time was making preparations for her forthcoming marriage to a soldier. Several weeks later, when George Cornwallis-West and his sister were looking through a collection of prints of Nell Gwynne, Daisy Cornwallis-West remarked on the resemblance between the former king's famous mistress and Ellen Bryan, and the soldier realised that it must have been Nell that he saw that day in the entrance hall.

A sequel to this event took place sometime later. Interested in psychometry – the practice of divining information from inanimate objects such as watches, jewellery and other personal items – George Cornwallis-West, withholding his true identity, visited a medium and during the course of the sitting handed the psychic a handwritten letter inside an envelope. He was told that the writer had recently seen the apparition of the mistress of Charles II and that she was attempting to warn him of some impending personal problem that had yet to take place. A short time after, Cornwallis-West's solicitor, a previously trusted employee, absconded with over £10,000 of his client's money, seeming confirmation of the psychic's sinister prediction several weeks before. A female apparition, again considered to be the ghost of Nell Gwynne, has been seen over the years in other places inside

The Green Bedroom at Salisbury Hall, where former owner Walter Goldsmith claimed to have encountered the presence of an unseen person. (Peter Underwood Collection)

Salisbury Hall including the main staircase and near the entrance to the Green Bedroom, but not inside the bedroom itself. However, Walter Goldsmith always regarded this particular bedroom as being a haunted part of the house and claimed to have sensed the presence of an unseen person there on a number of occasions.

As well as the famous Nell Gwynne, an unidentified male ghost from the time of the English Civil War is also said to haunt the house, having been both seen and heard on a number of occasions. This is a Cavalier, who according to a traditional account, was carrying dispatches in the area when he was intercepted by a party of Cromwell's soldiers and fled on horseback to the Salisbury estate in a desperate attempt to evade capture. However, although he

made it inside the house, the unnamed Royalist became trapped in the upper part of the building and with the Parliamentarians approaching, decided to take his own life rather than die at the hands of the enemy. Colourful accounts, such as this tale evoking the drama of this turbulent period of English history are often encountered by ghost hunters in allegedly haunted locations around the country. Here at Salisbury Hall, the ghostly Cavalier is said to have appeared several times over a period of many years. Although reports of the apparition manifesting with the blade of a sword sticking out of its torso would seem to be a continuation of the dramatic storytelling, footsteps have also been heard passing along an upper corridor into a bathroom which at one time would have been the route into the old Tudor wing of the house – Mrs Goldsmith claimed to have heard them during the 1960s. A male apparition, thought to be that of the long-dead Cavalier, was seen at least twice within living memory, both times by named witnesses. In the 1930s, Lady Gresley became terrified when an apparition entered her bedroom as she lay resting one evening and was so upset that she never slept in that room again.

Nearer to our own times in the 1970s, the Cavalier made another appearance, this time in the former coach house on the estate. One summer evening, around half past ten, Robin Goldsmith – Walter Goldsmith's son – and his future wife Maria were chasing each other around the old coach house building when suddenly Maria came face to face with a tall male figure that she later felt could only have been the long-dead Royalist's ghost. Maria Goldsmith described the apparition as being dressed in a white frill-fronted shirt, knee breeches and dark shoes, each with a shiny silver buckle. The man wore his long hair tied back with a ribbon and there was nothing sinister about his appearance. For several seconds the living and the dead seemed to gaze at one another, then the figure appeared to grow hazy and gradually faded away. After their marriage, the Goldsmiths lived for a time in Nell Gwynne's cottage which, after the departure of the de Havillands in 1947, had been used as a silkworm factory supplying the silk for the wedding dress and coronation robes of Queen Elizabeth II in 1947 and 1953 respectively.

Another room in the main house at Salisbury Hall with ghostly associations is a small bedroom over the entrance porch, used for many years as a children's nursery. An unidentified figure that emerges from a point close to the fireplace and crosses the room to stand at the bedside is said to have frightened several sleeping youngsters as well as, on separate occasions, two of the adult staff. One of these, a governess, spent a night in the nursery around the time of the Great War and subsequently refused to sleep there again – she described seeing a dark shape come towards her out of the wall next to the chimney breast. It was at this point during his initial refurbishment work on the building in the 1950s that Walter Goldsmith discovered a bricked-up doorway leading into another part of the house. It is a common fact that stone tape apparitions and ghostly figures often appear to trace the paths of former building layouts that, in time, have been altered or changed in some way, passing through – as in this case –a door opening that has become blocked, or following the original level of a floor or staircase that has at some later time in the building's history been raised or lowered (see the experience of Harry Martindale at the Treasurer's House at York as described in *Haunted Luton and Dunstable*). Although Robin Goldsmith slept in the haunted nursery for several years as a child and experienced nothing out of the ordinary, his fiancée had a particularly unpleasant night there during the time that they were preparing for their wedding. Waking in the early hours at around two o'clock, Maria Goldsmith noticed that a clock which had been stopped to prevent its loud ticking from disturbing her sleep was now working again and that the room seemed to be filled with what she described as a 'malevolent atmosphere'. As she lay awake, the bedstead suddenly became animated and started rocking backwards and forwards. Scared to get out of bed, the young woman buried her head in the bedclothes and eventually went back to sleep, although the strange vibrations continued for some time. Maria Goldsmith, who it seems had some natural psychic ability, had felt uneasy about the room the very first time she had stepped inside.

Contrasting with the sinister atmosphere of the old nursery is the unusual phenomenon associated with the grounds of Salisbury Hall, where ghost hunter Tony Broughall reports the rich laugh of a woman being heard on a number of occasions when the gardens have ostensibly been empty of visitors. Perhaps this is another psychic echo of the world of Charles II and Nell Gwynne and the times they spent together? Now in private ownership and no longer open to the public, Salisbury Hall remains one of the most interesting haunted houses of England.

5

SOME ANECDOTAL HAUNTINGS IN BRIEF

IN the opening part of this book we briefly touched on the concept of making ghost hunting a 'respectable' profession and the efforts by researchers and investigators to find explanations for the strange happenings that are experienced by many, but are still currently dismissed or reinterpreted by conventional orthodoxy and the scientific mainstream. The subject of the paranormal is in fact a divided one, not only in the broad sense between sceptics and believers, but also divided within itself. Most people like a good ghost story, and here in England we have an enviable tradition of some of the greatest examples of the genre, from writers such as M.R. James, E.F. Benson, Algernon Blackwood, Robert Aickman, and many others. I admit to being both intrigued and terrified at the same time by the BBC television adaptation of James' *Lost Hearts* in the early 1970s, a period when some of the finest interpretations of the writer's stories were being made, and which are now available to enjoy again on DVD. However, the sensational side of the paranormal – a subject which has always by its very nature leant itself to exploitation – is perhaps psychical research's greatest enemy, as it is too easy to dismiss genuine paranormal encounters as 'a good ghost story' and ignore what are perhaps the most challenging experiences that we as human beings can face in terms of their implications for both our past and present.

Many reports of ghosts and haunting are sadly lacking in terms of verifiable information – dates, names of witnesses and other corroborative evidence – and as such are easily and unsympathetically dismissed by the sceptic. Before we take a ghost walk around the streets of St Albans, it is worth looking at a number of other sites that help to make up the city's impressive quota of ghosts and haunted places, but for which many details are unavailable. Many are no doubt good stories, but all stories, it would seem, have a germ of truth in them, so in an attempt at completeness (or rather an attempt at giving a full picture of the ghostly side of the city of St Albans), the following brief accounts of some other haunted locations are included. This is a case where reader discretion is to be advised.

In Anglo-Saxon times, a royal fortified settlement known as the burgh of Kingsbury was established on land close to the abbey of St Alban. A large fishpond – now long since gone – that at one time provided the inhabitants of Kingsbury with food survives in the name of Fishpool Street, which winds its way along the north-east edge of the Verulamium between Romeland Hill and Branch Road. A number of the buildings, as well as the roadway itself, are reputed to have paranormal associations. A first floor bedroom in the seventeenth-century Lower Red Lion Inn is said to be haunted by the apparition of an unknown woman, as well as the unsettling sound of a crying child.

The mysterious movement of the bedsteads has also been reported along with a shadowy figure, said to appear on occasion in the ground floor tap room. Several private houses in Fishpool Street have their own ghosts which include two female apparitions: one seems friendly, while the other is a rather unpleasant spirit that tries to place its hands around the necks of the owners as they lie in bed at night. There is also the figure of a man in grey, and perhaps one of the oddest of all reported paranormal happenings: a disappearing window, or more accurately parts of a window, which are said to have vanished and then returned after a period of several weeks. One house, formerly The Angel Inn, is said to have a haunted cellar where the apparition of a Cavalier has been encountered on occasion in the past. At night time,

Fishpool Street, where several ghosts, including a phantom carriage and the apparition of a crying woman, are said to appear after dark. (Eddie Brazil)

The Red Lion Inn, Fishpool Street. Shadowy figures and the mysterious moving and shaking of bedsteads have been reported here in the past. (Eddie Brazil)

the street itself seems to come alive with a number of distinctive and unusual phantoms: they include the apparition of a Colonial-style post-chaise drawn by two white ponies with the figures of a man in a Panama hat and a woman in a blue dress on the box, another man in a tall stove-pipe hat, and the unhappy shade of a crying woman haranguing herself for the death of her child, accidentally smothered to death in the eighteenth century.

We have already discussed Holywell Hill earlier in our survey and looked at a number of its most interesting ghosts. In addition to these, we find several other anecdotal hauntings which include an unnamed house where both the presence, as well as the footsteps, of a phantom woman known as Granny Sheldrake have been experienced. Interestingly, the sound of her heavy tread is said to be most prevalent when young people – particularly children – are present, in much the same way that poltergeist activity can often be catalysed in households where young teenagers are living. Without further information or the opportunity to carry out a detailed examination, the case of Granny Sheldrake remains an enigmatic one. White Hart Cottage, close to the junction with Sumpter Yard, is one named building with paranormal associations but unlike Granny Sheldrake, the identity of a female apparition, seen many years ago by former resident Mrs Perkins, remains unknown. This Elizabethan-style apparition – complete with a white neck ruff and dark-coloured skull cap – was seen in one of the bedrooms, but nothing of a similar nature appears to have made itself known in recent times or occurred with any regularity to make the haunting more well-known.

One of two legend-type hauntings familiar to ghost hunters from many locations around the country is also represented on Holywell Hill: the spectral 'death coach' which, together with the phantom dog or black hound of death, makes up one of our most traditional native ghosts. In *Haunted Luton and Dunstable*, I looked at a number of examples of the black dog phenomenon in connection with the haunting of Galley Hill on the north-east outskirts of the town. There are many reports and stories of phantom coaches from varied locations across Britain, several of which are cyclical hauntings, associated with a specific place and day of the year. On 19 May, a spectral coach pulled by headless horses and carrying the ghost of Anne Boleyn drives towards Blickling Hall in Norfolk, the family home of the Boleyn family in the sixteenth century. Anne sits inside, with her head on her lap, and the whole vision rises into the air when it reaches the house and then fades away. The night of 31 May is a busy one where phantom coach hauntings are concerned. A mustard-coloured coach driven by the Duke de Morrow is said to career down the driveway of Hill Hall near Theydon Bois in Essex, an Elizabethan mansion subsequently used in the second half of the twentieth century as a women's prison before being refurbished into apartments. At Potter Heigham in Norfolk, at the stroke of midnight, a ghostly coach with sparks flying from its wheels is said to cross the old bridge over the River Thurne before crashing and disappearing into the water, while over in County Antrim, a black coach is associated with the ruins of Massereene Castle on the shores of Lough Neagh in Northern Ireland. On Christmas Eve, another ghostly coach-and-four, this time with a headless groom on the box, rides to the entrance of the sixteenth-century Roos Hall on the outskirts of Beccles in Suffolk, considered by some to be the most haunted house in East Anglia. A few days later, on New Year's Eve, when the water of the Loch of Skene in Aberdeenshire is frozen, another ghostly carriage is said to appear and cross from one side to the other. Although the most famous Christmas ghosts are those created by Charles Dickens, there are many real-life hauntings around Britain that are associated with this particular time of the year. A convincing cyclical haunting that I have personally experienced took place in a terraced house in Second Avenue in Emsworth, West Sussex during the 1990s, where the apparition of a man was seen in an upstairs room; more interestingly, however, were the mysterious smoke-like shapes and other anomalies that appeared on ordinary photographs taken inside the house during the Christmas period. This was a complex case that has never been fully investigated or explained. The most famous phantom coach, however, is undoubtedly the one said to have appeared a number of times to named witnesses in the grounds of the notorious Borley Rectory in Essex: it was seen by the Revd Harry Bull, the incumbent whose father built the rectory in the early 1860s, and who died in the eerie-sounding Blue Room in the house in 1927. It was later also seen by Edward Cooper, who lived with his wife in the Rectory Cottage during and shortly after the First World War. At Holywell Hill in St Albans, the phantom coach is, like its counterpart at Blicking Hall, said to be pulled by headless horses, while the fact that its supposed appearances are associated with the roadway outside the White Hart Hotel shows that its origins may lie in the case of the unfortunate Elizabeth Wilson, whose death outside the building we have already mentioned in an earlier part of this book.

On the north-west outskirts of St Albans are another two allegedly haunted locations. Batchwood Hall, now a nightclub, was built by Edmund Beckett, who as we have seen, has an important association with the great abbey church. During refurbishment work in the late 1980s, a number of unusual incidents of a paranormal nature were reported by building contractors: these included the movement of objects, padlocks being unlocked, and lights seemingly turning on and off by themselves. The apparition of a woman scattering burning coals from a shovel is also associated with the building. A short distance from Batchwood Hall, on the A5183 Redbourn Road, is the Pré hotel and restaurant, where the sounds of footsteps walking down empty corridors and ghostly knocking noises on some of the bedroom doors have allegedly been reported by members of staff. The hotel is said to be haunted by the apparition of Isobel Toulmin, who lived there as a child in the late 1800s. During the month of August, the figure of a child is said to appear in photographs taken by guests at the hotel and the appearance of a vision of Saint Alban wearing white robes and surrounded by a glow of golden light – seen by Isobel Toulmin herself – is also associated with the site.

Olfactory phenomena, i.e. phantom smells and odours, are another curious happening sometimes encountered in haunted buildings. They range from the pleasant scent of flowers and perfume, unusual smells such as candle grease and cooking food to the macabre odours of open graves and decaying flesh. During the mid-1990s, I worked in an early seventeenth-century detached house in Millmead in Guildford, Surrey, where as well as the phantom sound of people moving about on the upper floors – experienced several times by staff working in the building after hours – the odour of cigar smoke was often encountered on the staircase at odd times of the day, most often in the early morning. At Sandford Orcas Manor House near Sherborne in Dorset, a former tenant, Colonel Claridge, told me about the ghost they called the 'stinking man', whose footsteps through the staff wing towards the gatehouse were accompanied by an unusual dragging noise and the smell of rotting bodies. At the Pemberton Almshouses in St Peter's Street, St Albans, the ghostly smell reported on occasion by a former occupant was more mundane rather than terrifying. The building dates from the 1620s and was built by a former High Sheriff of Hertfordshire, Roger Pemberton. Here the odour of tobacco smoke would on occasion fill the entire house, even though the woman who is said to have experienced the phenomenon was a non-smoker and lived there alone.

The unsettling sound of human screams must be one of the most frightening paranormal experiences. At an unidentified house in Wellclose Street only a short walk from much haunted Fishpool Street, the family of a BBC producer were forced to call in the services of an exorcist after they were disturbed in the night on a number of occasions by the sound of a woman screaming. The disturbances are said to have taken place in the 1950s and were accompanied by the appearance of a Victorian-looking woman who was seen in one of the bedrooms as well as walking down a corridor, and on one

occasion peering in through a kitchen window; knocks and other rapping-type noises were also heard. The house was at one time used as a nursery, and the haunting was said to have been caused by the ghost of a former owner who was recognised as being the face at the window from a painting found by the owner. Another female apparition is said to haunt the garden of a house in nearby Verulam Road, while in St Michael's Street the former Sally Lunn tearoom, St Alban's oldest residential building, also has a ghostly lady. Former members of staff claim to have seen the apparition of a middle-aged woman in a white dress on a number of occasions. She was often encountered on the staircase early in the morning, and workers complained of a feeling of being watched while alone in certain parts of the building. A former Sister is said to haunt parts of St Albans Hospital on dark winter evenings, while the apparition of an old woman working on her embroidery is one of several ghosts to have walked an old house known as The Gables and located at the entrance to French Row close to the old clock tower. The figure of an unidentified man apparently haunted a storeroom in the upper part of this building; objects were often found to have been moved around during the time the premises were closed up and locked for the night.

The sound of human footsteps is perhaps the most commonly reported paranormal phenomenon in haunted buildings, and there are a number of examples included in the cases in the present survey. It is perhaps fitting to close this brief tour of the anecdotal hauntings of St Albans with a visit to the site of the old prison in Grimston Road, where the footfalls of a long-dead warder were at one time said to walk the gravelled courtyard. This was after the prison's closure in 1924, when it was being used by St Albans Council as a depot, by which time large sections of the old building had been demolished. The prison opened in 1867, following the closure of the haunted Abbey Gateway that we have already encountered earlier in this book, and was known as a hanging prison: four executions took place here, the last being that of George Anderson who was hanged by John Ellis and George Brown on 23 December 1914. Today the St Albans Registry Office occupies the former governor's residence, which is the only part of the old jail still standing.

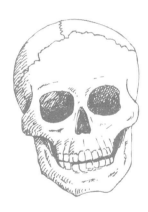

6

A ST ALBANS GHOST WALK

OUR survey of St Albans' haunted heritage comes to a close with a suggestion for a ghost walk around parts of the city centre, picking up a number of sites with paranormal connections along the way. The walk starts and finishes at the medieval clock tower in the Market Place, and covering 2.5 miles, would take around an hour and a half to complete in total at a leisurely pace: ideal for a Sunday morning, or if you feel brave enough, on an evening (at a brisk pace) when the light is failing and the compelling world of the unseen seems to be that much closer to our own. However, if you don't have the time for a ghost hunting marathon, the route falls into two loops which can be walked separately. This neatly divides the tour into two sections, the first concentrating on Fishpool Street and the Abbey Church, the second focusing on St Peter's Street.

The figures in brackets correspond with a location marked on the map. Nearly all of the haunted stops along the way are included in the main part of the book and it is worth taking a camera with

you as spontaneous encounters with the paranormal can happen, as we have seen, when you least expect them …

Starting with the clock tower behind you, turn right into the High Street. The building on the immediate corner of the junction with Market Place was once known as (1) The Gables, where at least two apparitions have been seen: the figure of an 'evil-looking' man, and an old woman doing embroidery. Continue down the High Street and pass the Heritage Close shopping arcade on your left. At the junction with George Street is the former (2) Tudor Tavern, now a Thai restaurant, where a shadowy figure – considered by some to be the ghost of a casualty from the First Battle of St Albans – has been reported following members of staff. Keep left into George Street and head down the hill. Continue on into Romeland Hill. On the elevated pavement on the left where the roadway turns down towards the abbey is a line of white houses known as the site of (3) Romeland Cottage, where the apparition of a cowled figure was seen on

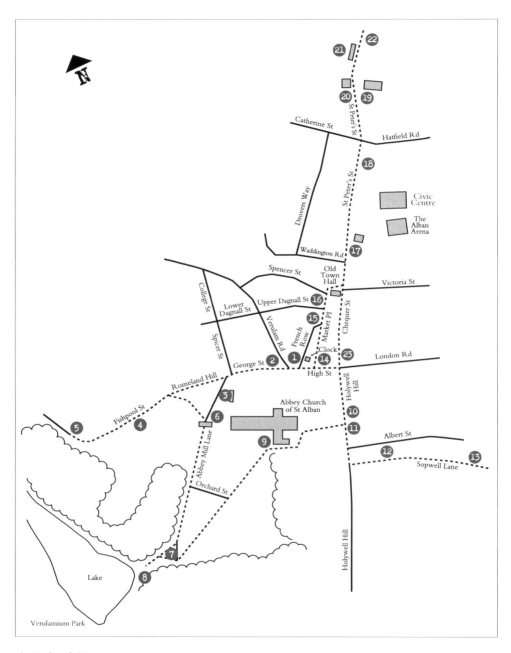

A plan for a St Albans ghost walk.

several occasions by a family maid in the years before the First World War. Stay in Romeland Hill and follow it down into the attractive and much haunted (4) Fishpool Street. Here there are many allegedly haunted buildings, and if you are doing this walk at night, there are a number of phantom figures including a crying woman, a man wearing a tall hat and the vision of a horse-drawn carriage, that are said to haunt the roadway itself during the hours of darkness. Stroll down to the (5) Lower Red Lion Inn, where the apparition of a young woman has been seen in one of the bedrooms and the sad sound of a crying child has been heard, before retracing your steps up Fishpool Street and following the road to the right at the junction with Romeland Hill. This will lead you to the imposing (6) Abbey Gateway, once used as the city prison and now part of St Albans School. Here the sounds of screaming men have been heard and there are reports of the building's windows opening and closing by themselves.

Walk through the great archway and head down into Abbey Mill Lane. At the bottom of the hill is (7) Ye Olde Fighting Cocks, the oldest public house in St Albans and one of the oldest hostelries in the country. Here the apparitions of monk-like figures have been observed emerging from the cellar and objects have been mysteriously moved around. At the end of Abbey Mill Lane, adjacent to the Fighting Cocks, is the pedestrian bridge over the River Ver into (8) Verulamium Park, known to ghost hunters as the haunt of ghostly Roman soldiers as well as the apparition of a Civil War Cavalier, so it is worth spending some time here taking in the scenery, although the park's ghosts appear to have

only materialised at night so far. Re-cross the River Ver bridge and turn to the right. With the pub on your left, take the paved footpath at the end of Abbey Mill Lane that cuts in a north-east direction across a wide area of open parkland. Soon you will reach the impressive (9) Abbey Church of St Alban, now most often called St Albans Cathedral. During the Second World War, a local fire-watcher claimed to have encountered the apparitions of phantom monks, and the sounds of matins being sung by ghostly voices appear to have imprinted themselves in some way on the stonework of this ancient building. Robed figures have also been seen here during the daytime, so keep an eye out as you walk past.

Walking around the Abbey Church in a clockwise direction will eventually bring you to Sumpter Yard, a short pedestrian road on the east side of the cathedral. Follow this to the end, where it joins (10) Holywell Hill, one of St Albans' most haunted streets. Directly opposite Sumpter Yard is the (11) White Hart Hotel, where in 1820 a woman riding on the top of a coach was killed when her head struck the archway in front of you. She is just one of the ghosts said to haunt this attractive building; there are also reports of the apparition of a little girl as well as phantom writing appearing inside, together with the paranormal movement of objects. Holywell Hill is known for a number of ghosts, including the apparition of a woman holding a wicker basket and the sounds of a phantom battle, said to be the paranormal soundtrack of the First Battle of St Albans that was fought in this part of the city in 1455. From Sumpter Yard, turn right down the hill and take the second turning into Sopwell Lane on the left. Along this road you will find two haunted pubs that make convenient stopping points: (12) The Goat Inn, where a strange atmosphere has been noted by several people and a former landlord experienced the movement of objects and the vision of a disturbing face that appeared in one of the first floor rooms, and (13) The White Lion, said to be haunted by the ghost of a young woman who waits in vain for the return of her lover, who unbeknown to her, was executed on the gallows. Now retrace your steps back along Sopwell Lane, turn right into Holywell Hill and follow it up to the crossroads junction. A left turn into the High Street will take you back to the clock tower and the completion of the first section of the ghost walk.

The second part of our ghost tour takes in a number of haunted locations along St Peter's Street to the north. Directly opposite the clock tower is (14) The Boot Inn, where poltergeist-type interference with lighting and electrical equipment has been reported in the past. Walk up the Market Place until you reach the spot where the road and French Row converge. On the left is the entrance to the Christopher Place shopping centre. The building on the right of the archway, currently an optician's, is the site of the former (15) Wellington public house, at one time one of St Albans' most haunted buildings. Footsteps and poltergeist activity were reported here as well as the appearance of insubstantial apparitions when the premises were used as a butcher's shop during

Site of the former Charnel House, where some residue from former times may still linger on. (Eddie Brazil)

the 1970s. Continue along the Market Place until you reach the junction with Upper Dagnall Street on the left. The building on the corner, for many years a branch of W.H. Smith, is where the (16) Charnel House once stood. The Charnel Brotherhood, an early governing body, held their meetings here in the sixteenth century following the Dissolution of the Monasteries. The building is known to have been haunted in the past when lights were reported to turn themselves on and off.

Walk along the last part of the Market Place until you reach the junction with St Peter's Street, passing the old Town Hall building on your right, at one time thought to be the site of the trial of rebel leader John Ball in 1381. Cross over the road and continue left up St Peter's Street, where soon you will pass (17) The Grange on your right, now a branch of the Nationwide building society. This building has a haunted reputation stretching back to the time it was used as offices by St Albans Council during the 1940s, and there are reports of the figure of a woman in a grey dress being seen in one of the first-floor corridors in recent years. Carry on along St Peter's Street until you come to Mallinson House, a large three-storey double-fronted house with a portico entrance directly opposite the pedestrian alleyway to Adelaide Street on the other side of the road. Originally known as (18) Donnington House, the residence of a former St Albans doctor, it was the scene of a disturbance in 1872 when a large crowd of several hundred people waited to see the reappearance of a ghostly figure that had been reported in one of the upper-floor windows.

Carry on along St Peter's Street to the roundabout junction with Hatfield Road. At one time, bones discovered in the cellar of The Cock Inn on the corner were thought to have been the finger bones of casualties of the St Albans battles of the Wars of the Roses, but today they are considered to be of animal origin. Cross the road and walk further up the street until you come to (19) St Peter's Church on the right. Here, the sighting of a male apparition in 1258 climbing the tower is thought to be the city's earliest reported ghost. On the opposite side of the road is (20) Ivy House, where previous occupants have encountered the apparition of a sad-faced young woman, thought to be a former servant. The ghost was reported to appear around Christmas time, but apparently has not been seen for several years. Walk further up St Peter's Street until you come to the (21) Pemberton Almshouses on the opposite side of the road. Here, unusual smells have been reported in the past, which were thought to have a paranormal origin. Just past the almshouses on the right is the site of the former (22) Hall Place Mansion, which was demolished in the early 1900s. During the Wars of the Roses, the building was used by King Henry VI, and there is a local tradition that his ghost was seen here at times stepping out of the walls.

Now retrace your steps back down St Peter's Street until you reach the Old Town Hall and carry on into Chequer Street. On the left hand side, just before the junction with the High Street, is the site of the old (23) Battlefield House, now occupied by a pub/restaurant chain. Here the ghostly sounds of fighting men, thought to be

The Abbey Church of St Alban, on the south-western approach to the fifth most haunted city in England. (Eddie Brazil)

a psychic replay of the First Battle of St Albans, were reported over the years as well as the sound of chanting monks. Turn right into the High Street and you will soon be back to the starting point at the old clock tower, completing the short tour of this historic and seemingly much-haunted city.

7

ASSESSING ST ALBANS' GHOSTS

OUR survey of St Albans' paranormal history has shown that this, the fifth most haunted city in the United Kingdom, has a broad range of ghostly phenomena to its credit: haunting apparitions, paranormal singing and music, time-slip ghosts, strange atmospheres, cyclical hauntings and the supernormal movement of objects have all been reported here over the years, the one exception being a 'classic' poltergeist case such as those occurring at Pontefract in the 1960s and at Enfield in North London in 1977, although it is conceivable that such a disturbance may have taken place at some time in the past and subsequently gone unreported. As one interesting paranormal statistic states that some form of poltergeist activity is occurring within 3 miles of where you are currently reading this book, perhaps just such a phenomenon might be taking place at this very moment ...

With such a long and impressive social history, together with a wealth of old and attractive buildings, perhaps it is no surprise that St Albans rates so highly in the paranormal hit parade. During the course of compiling this survey, I have been struck with the anecdotal nature of a number of the cases under review, a fact that tends to reduce the quality of the material to a great extent. Seeing as it has been suggested that only 2 per cent of psychic happenings have a genuine supernormal content, the number of true ghost sightings and hauntings said to have taken place here may well be considerably reduced in number. It would seem reasonable, however, to tread some kind of middle ground where the ghosts of St Albans are concerned, and suggest that the real number of genuine psychic happenings in the city are not as many as have been listed, but are far more than one would normally expect to encounter in the average town or built-up area across the country. If one considers the atmospheric photograph or stone tape theory as a reasonable working hypothesis for explaining reports of ghostly figures and similar paranormal activity, then it would seem highly likely that a city teeming with so many historic houses, buildings and ancient roadways will also be teeming with strange and mysterious replays of its eventful and, at times, violent past.

Spontaneous paranormal activity is perhaps the most convincing form of unexplained phenomena that the psychical researcher may encounter, and it can take place seemingly anywhere and without warning. During the time that this book was being compiled in the summer and autumn of 2012, just such activity began in the house of a friend of mine. Like many such cases, it remains puzzling and completely inexplicable. It serves as a good example to round off this collection of strange and mysterious happenings.

Jane Jones [pseudonym] lived at the time with her Brazilian-born husband and their two young children, Lillian [pseudonym] aged 5 and Michael [pseudonym] aged 4, in a small terraced Victorian house in the High Town area of Luton, Bedfordshire. During the months of June and July, Jane often found one of her daughter's soft toys, a cuddly Eeyore from the popular Winnie the Pooh stories, lying discarded on the floor in the children's bedroom, but understandably thought nothing of it. One evening while running a bath for herself (Michael and Lillian having gone to bed), Jane went into the children's bedroom and again noticed the same toy lying on the floor between the two bedsteads; she picked it up and placed it on top of a chest of drawers and left the room. A few minutes later, on returning to check on the children, the same Eeyore toy was now back on the floor – both children were still sound asleep and in the same identical positions as they had been when she had tidied up only a few moments before.

A day or so later, Jane again went into the children's bedroom and noticed that several of her daughter's animal toys and figures had been neatly lined up on a shelf above Lillian's bed, each with their faces pointing towards the wall. Although it was conceivable that their daughter could have arranged the toys in such a way, the positioning of the figures was so out of character from the normal way that the child played with or left her playthings out around the house that their mother felt certain that the items had been placed in such a way as though something or someone was trying to draw attention to itself.

Things were to come to a head in the house the following morning. Both children had been playing with various toys in the ground-floor front room before being called upstairs. As she took both Lillian and Michael up to their bedroom, Jane Jones noticed that two of the soft toys were lying on the sofa. When she came downstairs and into the front room a few minutes later, the same two toys were now sitting on the top of a large wall clock on the spine wall facing the street door (the front door opened directly from the living room onto the pavement) with both their faces turned towards the wall in the same fashion as the row of toys had been arranged in the bedroom on the previous day. No one had been downstairs at the time, and neither child would have been able to reach the top of the clock even if they had stood on the sofa; it would also have been impossible to have thrown both toys so that they landed in the way they were found, neatly positioned, again as though whatever was causing the disturbances wanted its activities to be noticed. Now unnerved by the various happenings, Jane and her husband spoke with their local Catholic priest who suggested blessing the house by sprinkling holy water in each of the rooms; this the couple duly did, and to date there have been no more incidents of a similar nature. The couple left the house a short time afterwards. It is also worth mentioning that a dog the couple regularly look after is often unwilling to spend time in the downstairs front room where the toys were moved, although it was quite at ease in the other rooms on the ground floor of the house. It is a well-known fact that both dogs and cats are psychically sensitive animals and often react to things that are not seen or felt by ordinary people.

How are we to explain this brief but nevertheless intriguing series of events? To some, the odd movement of simple items might seem a trivial occurrence, but for psychical researchers, like the great twentieth-century ghost hunter Harry Price whose Borley Rectory investigation has become one of the world's most famous ghost hunts, it was incidents such as this that were of the greatest importance: Price felt that the paranormal movement of a matchbox by just one inch was more impressive than a whole cavalcade of ghosts marching down the staircase of a stately home with their heads underneath their arms. I have no doubt in Jane Jones' sincerity in reporting the incidents described above, and that the toys moved in a 'supernormal' way. But how did they move? To the spiritualist, this phenomena would be the result of some activity involving discarnate 'entities' or spirit people – a friend of mine, a natural clairvoyant and developing physical medium, felt that a spirit child might be involved

and was wanting its presence to be made known to the family. It is true that there is a strong spiritualist connection in the family of Jane's husband: Brazil has a great spiritualist tradition: the teachings of Allan Kardec (1804-1869), a French educator and writer, have evolved into a specific branch of spiritualism known as Spiritism, and several of Jane's in-laws are psychically sensitive. To the parapsychologist, the spontaneous movement of objects is akin to some form of poltergeist phenomena, for which the most popular theory concerning its causation involves psychokinetic activity centred around the presence of an adolescent child, often a young teenage girl, but not exclusively so. It is true that in this particular case, all of the happenings seemed to be focused around Jane's five-year-old daughter Lillian; however, she falls completely outside the adolescent age-range normally associated with poltergeist activity. Another theory for the activities of the poltergeist is one that has been championed in the past by Guy Playfair, a well-respected and seasoned researcher with practical experience of a number of poltergeist cases both in this country and in Brazil, together with writer Colin Wilson. They both feel that the phenomena associated with poltergeist hauntings is caused by the activities of non-human 'entities' that live in a non-physical realm separate from our own material world, but who can draw 'energy' from certain sources (primarily the emotional forces associated with human puberty and adolescence) and create physical manifestations, including the movement of objects and other – at times – violent activity, including spontaneous fires, stone throwing and the occasional appearance of phantom figures and apparitions. I have no explanation for the strange happenings in Jane Jones' home – I only know that they happened.

Which brings us to the end of our survey of ghosts and hauntings in and around the city of St Albans. Clearly the twilight and mysterious realm of the paranormal is continually interacting with our own, wherever we are. Outside, there is mundane normality: rush-hour traffic, grey skies, noisy conversation, a mobile phone ringing; while inside, without warning, strange things outside of normality are taking place: a door opens on its own, footsteps sound in an empty corridor, a light comes on by itself, a toy is twitched off a shelf as if by an unseen hand, while something moves in a glimpse out of the corner of the eye, perhaps even as you glance up after reading this final page…

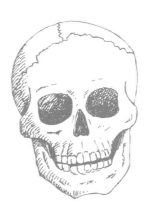

BIBLIOGRAPHY & FURTHER READING

Books

Adams, Paul, *Ghosts & Gallows: True Stories of Crime & the Paranormal* (The History Press, Stroud, 2012)

Adams, Paul, *Haunted Luton and Dunstable* (The History Press, Stroud, 2012)

Adams, Paul & Brazil, Eddie, *Extreme Hauntings: Britain's Most Terrifying Ghosts* (The History Press, Stroud, 2013)

Alexander, Marc, *Haunted Churches and Abbeys of Britain* (Arthur Barker, London, 1978)

Archer, Fred, *Exploring the Psychic World* (Paperback Library, New York, 1968)

Broughall, Tony & Adams, Paul, *Two Haunted Counties: A Ghost Hunter's Companion to Bedfordshire & Hertfordshire* (The Limbury Press, Luton, 2010)

Cabell, Craig, *Witchfinder General: The Biography of Matthew Hopkins* (Sutton Publishing, Stroud, 2006)

Freeman, Mark, *St Albans: A History* (Carnegie Publishing Ltd, Lancaster, 2008)

Gauld, Alan, *The Founders of Psychical Research* (Routledge & Kegan Paul, London, 1968)

Gurney, E., Myers, F.W.H. and Podmore, F., *Phantasms of the Living*, Vol. 1 & 2 (Trubner & Co., London, 1886)

King, William H., *Haunted Bedfordshire: A Ghostly Compendium* (The Book Castle, Dunstable, 2005)

Koestler, Arthur, *The Roots of Coincidence* (Random House, London, 1972)

Lethbridge, T.C., *Ghost and Ghoul* (Routledge and Kegan Paul, London, 1961);

Lethbridge, T.C., *Ghost and Divining Rod* (Routledge and Kegan Paul, London, 1963)

McEwan, Graham J., *Haunted Churches of England* (Robert Hale, London, 1989)

Moss, Peter, *Ghosts Over Britain* (Elm Tree Books, London, 1977)

O'Dell, Damien, *Paranormal Hertfordshire* (Amberley Publishing, Stroud, 2009)

Pelletier, Donald, *Mysterious Ruins: The Story of Sopwell Priory, St Albans* (The Book Castle, Dunstable, 2002)

Playfair, Guy Lyon, *The Haunted Pub Guide* (Harrap, London, 1985)

Puttick, Betty, *Ghosts of Hertfordshire* (Countryside Books, Newbury, 1994)

Puttick, Betty, *Supernatural England* (Countryside Books, Newbury, 2002)

Stratton, Ruth & Connell, Nick, *Haunted Hertfordshire: A Ghostly Gazetteer* (The Book Castle, Dunstable, 2006)

Thresher, Muriel & Carrington, Beryl, 'St Albans Ghost Lore' (St Albans & Hertfordshire Architectural & Archaeological Society, St Albans, 1987)

Underwood, Peter, *The Ghost Hunter's Guide* (Blandford Press, Poole, 1986)

Local Paranormal Groups

A Hertfordshire-based ghost-hunting organisation with an interest in St Albans hauntings is Damien O'Dell's Anglia Paranormal Investigation Society (APIS). APIS is always keen to involve serious-minded people with an interest in the paranormal in their investigations. Details can be found on their website: www.apisteamspirit.co.uk.

Based in neighbouring Bedfordshire, the Luton Paranormal Society (LPS) is a well-established investigative group with a yearly programme of visits to haunted locations throughout Buckinghamshire, Bedfordshire and Hertfordshire. There is an extensive database of local hauntings, including many St Albans cases on the society's website: www.lutonparanormal.com.

National Paranormal Organisations

For anyone involved in serious research into the paranormal, membership of the following three British societies should be considered. They are the Ghost Club (www.ghostclub.org.uk), founded in 1862; ASSAP, the Association for the Scientific Study of Anomalous Phenomena (www.assap.ac.uk), founded in 1981; and the SPR, the Society for Psychical Research (www.spr.ac.uk), established in 1882. Their publications and archives contain invaluable information and resource material, much of which is now being made available online.

If you enjoyed this book, you may also be interested in…

Haunted Luton & Dunstable
PAUL ADAMS

Paranormal historian Paul Adams leads you on a paranormal tour of Luton and Dunstable, recounting supernatural experiences such as apparitions on Galley Hill, the phantom hitch-hiker and the ghostly knights of Someries Castle. With rich illustrations and first-hand accounts, this book will fascinate anyone with an interest in the paranormal.

978 0 7524 6548 7

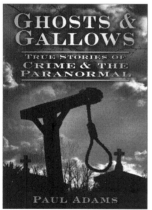

Ghosts & Gallows:
True Stories of Crime and the Paranormal
PAUL ADAMS

Vengeful spectres seeking justice or haunting the scene of the crime or their killers have adorned the pages of literature since before Shakespeare. This chilling collection of true-crime tales all feature some element of the paranormal, gathered from across the UK. This book is a fascinating look at criminology and ghost hunting.

978 0 7524 6339 1

Extreme Hauntings:
Britain's Most Terrifying Ghosts
PAUL ADAMS & EDDIE BRAZIL

Not for the faint of heart, this book explores the dark and disturbing world of the paranormal. Stories of deadly curses, violent poltergeists and spirit possession spanning more than 250 years from all over the UK are brought together by Paul Adams and Eddie Brazil in a detailed examination of extreme hauntings.

978 0 7524 6535 7

Visit our website and discover thousands of other History Press books.

www.thehistorypress.co.uk